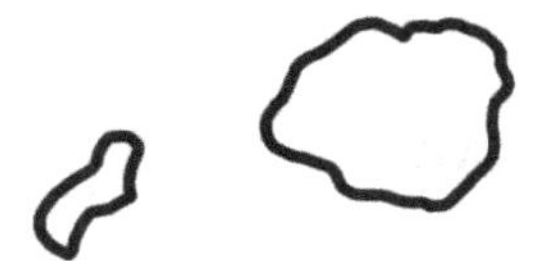

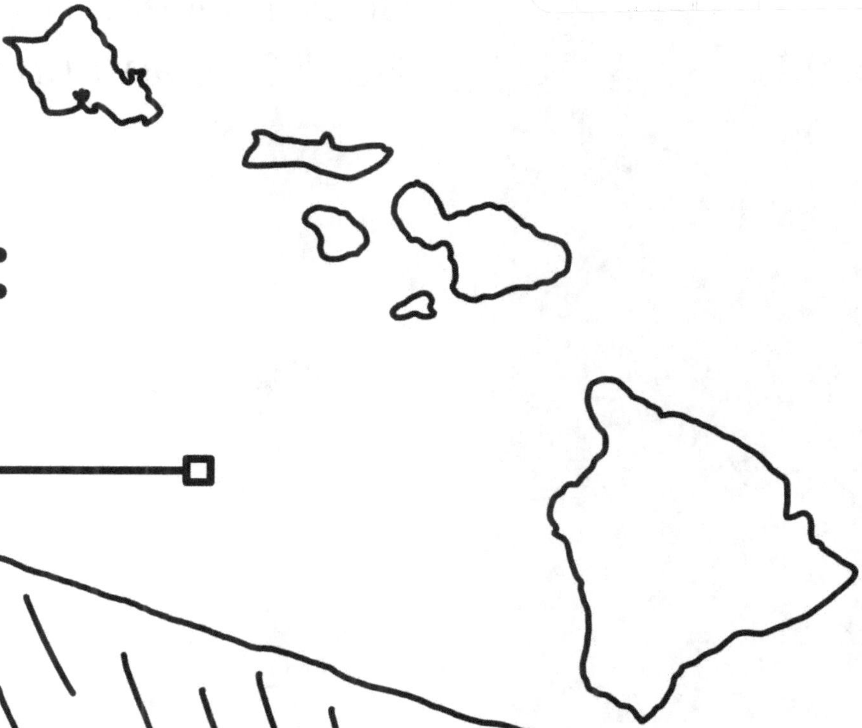

This book belongs to:

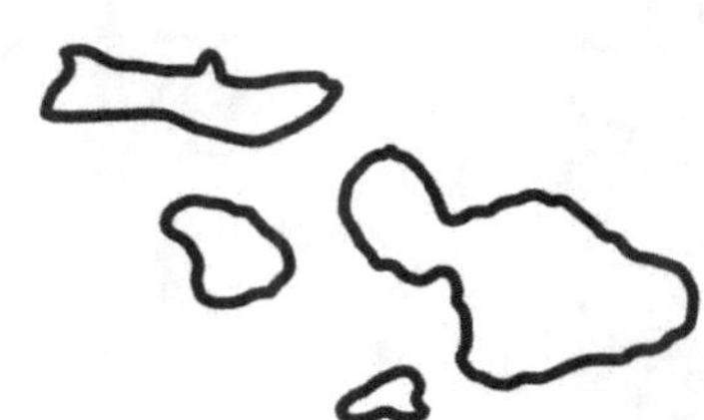

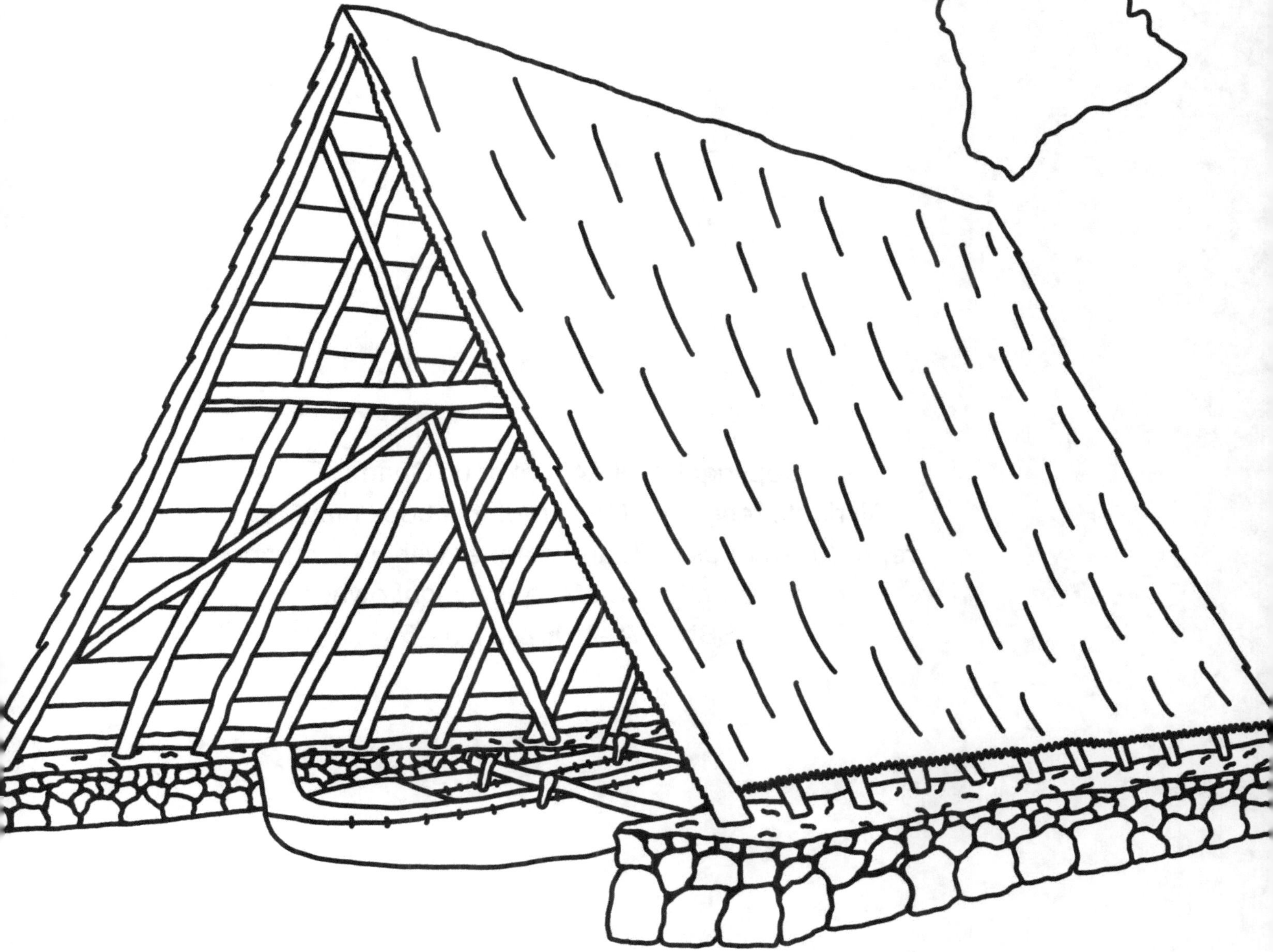

Color and Learn in ʻŌlelo Hawaiʻi Series
Book 1: Ocean Animals
Book 2: Island Animals

KŌLEA

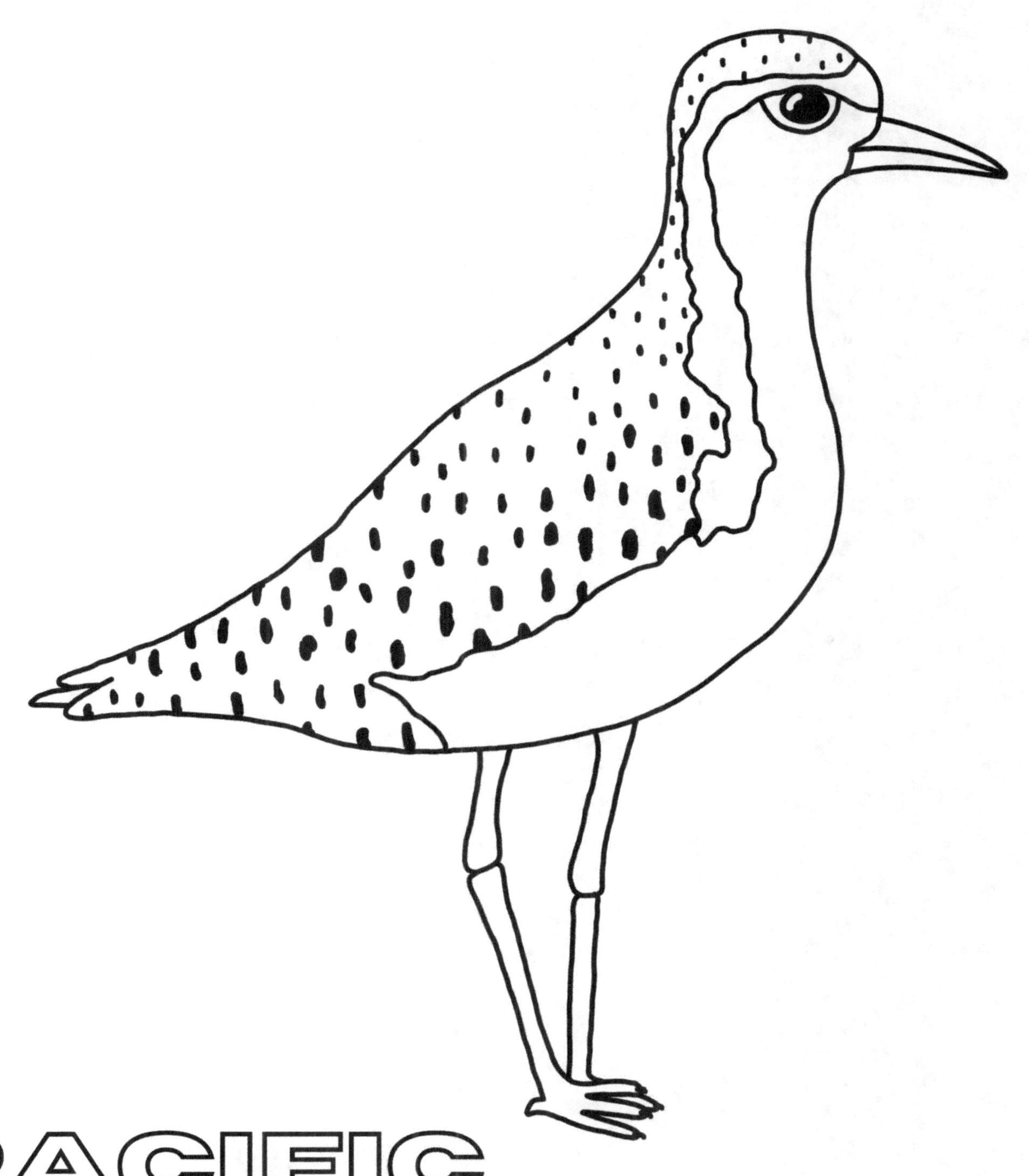

PACIFIC GOLDEN-PLOVER

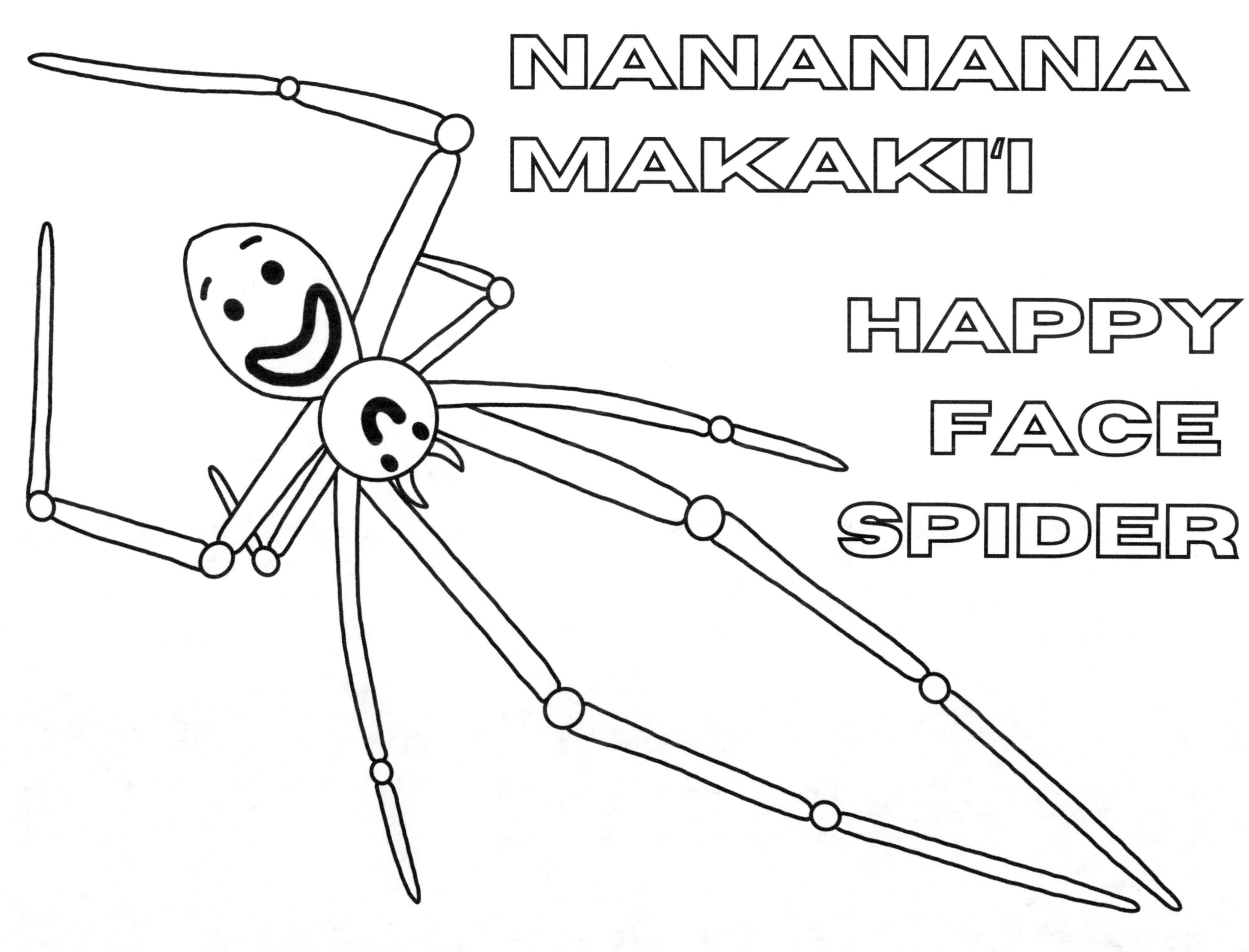

NANANANA
MAKAKI'I

HAPPY
FACE
SPIDER

HAWAIIAN HOARY BAT

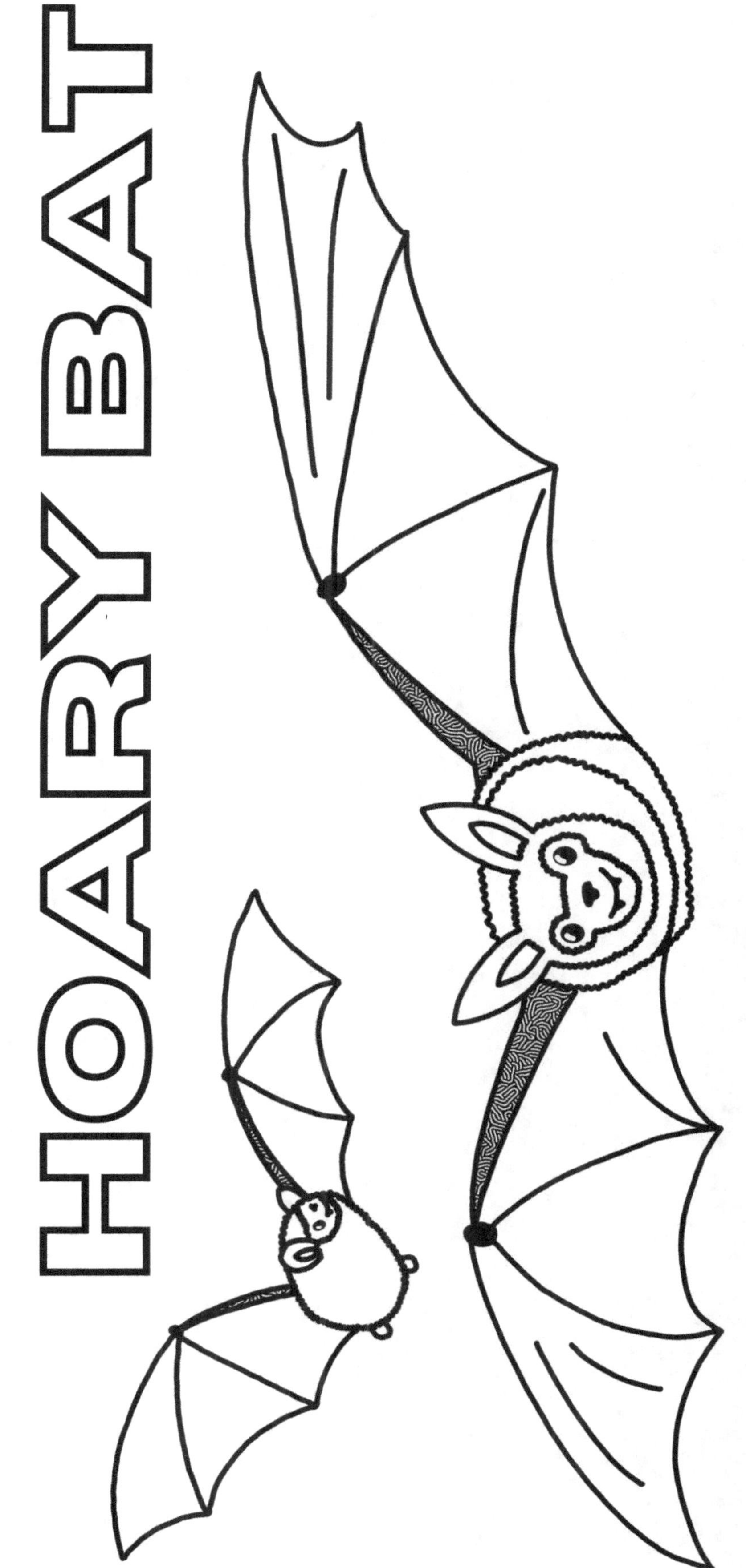

'ŌPE'APE'A

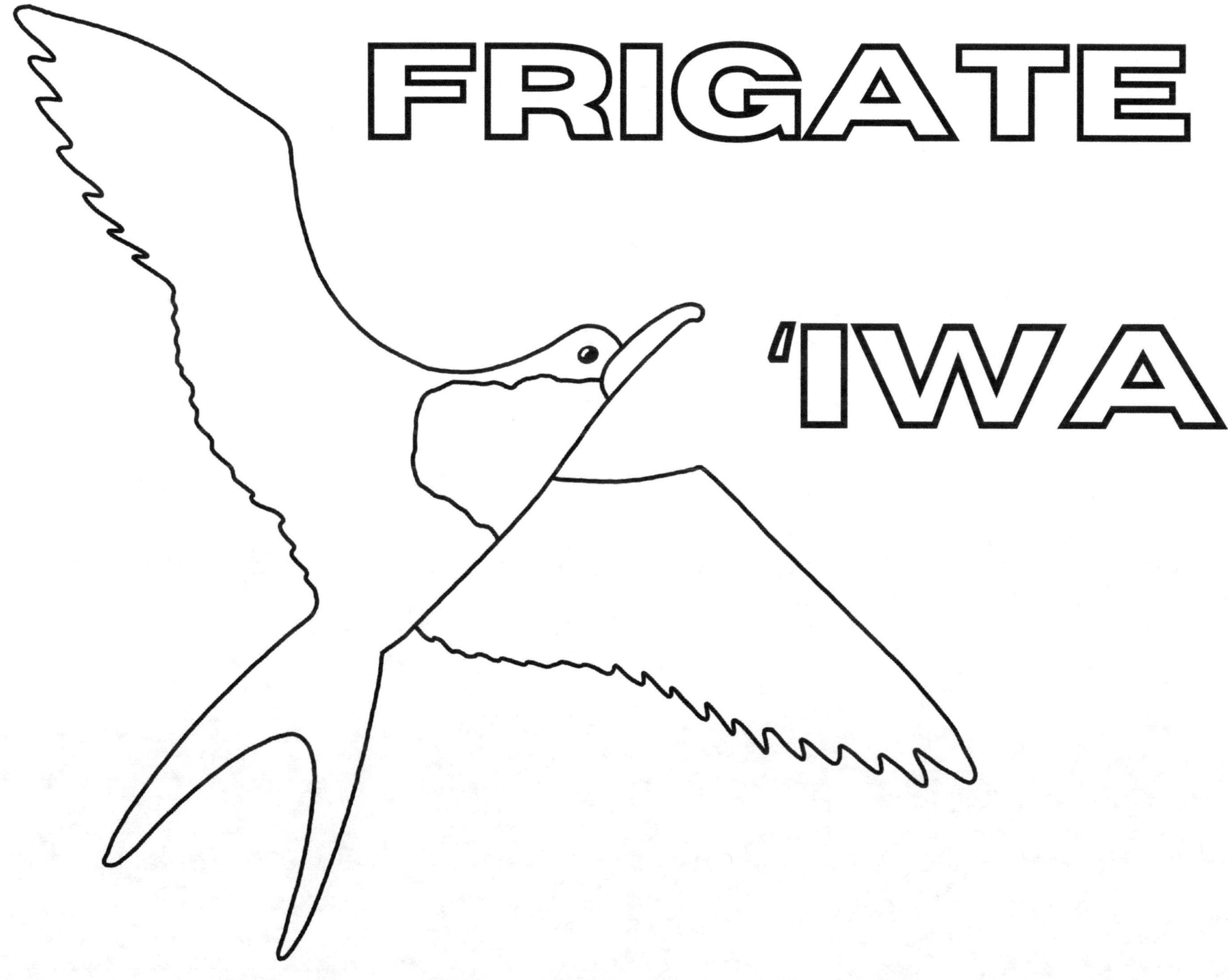

FRIGATE
'IWA

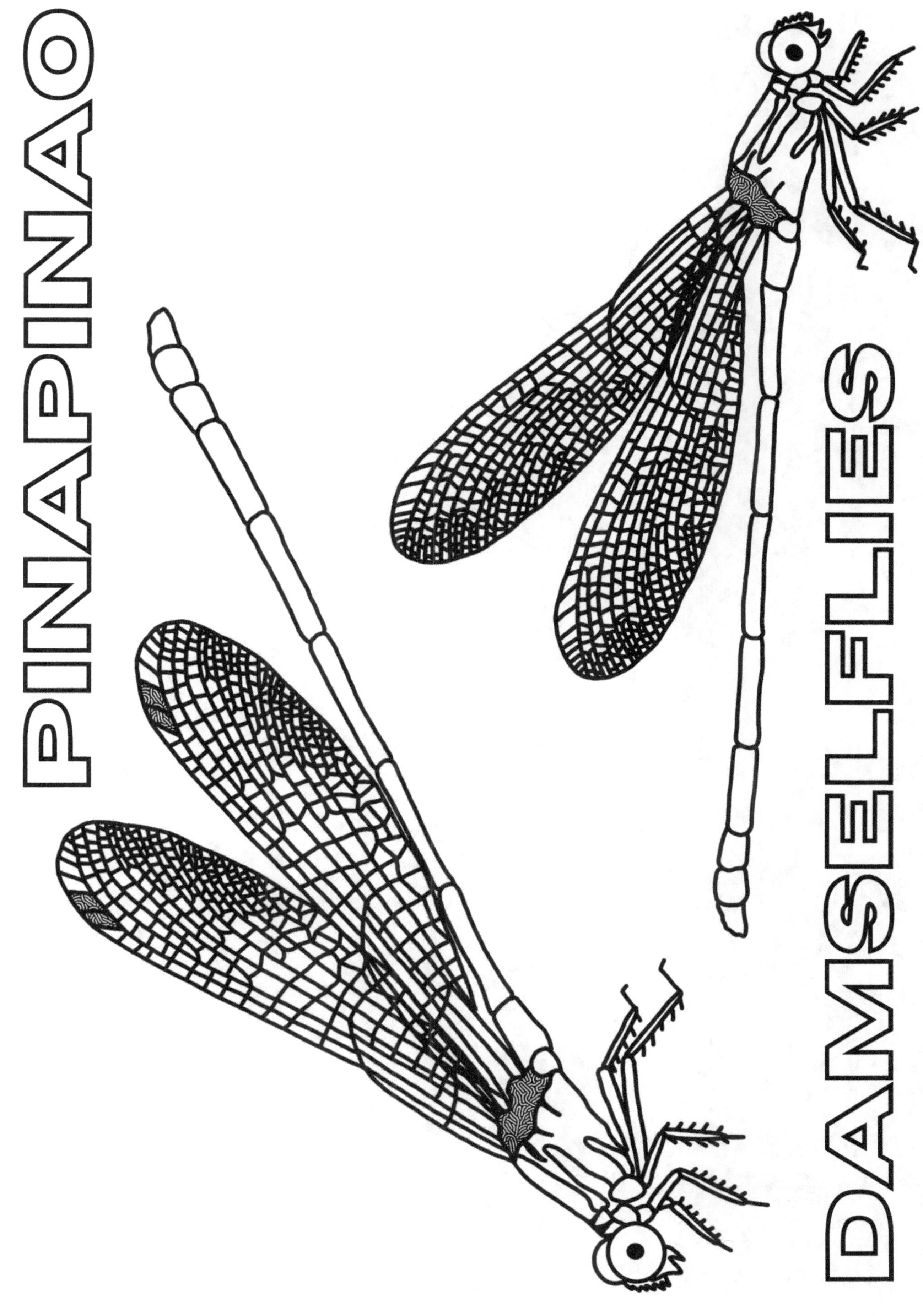

PINAPINAO
DAMSELFLIES

FRESHWATER GOBI

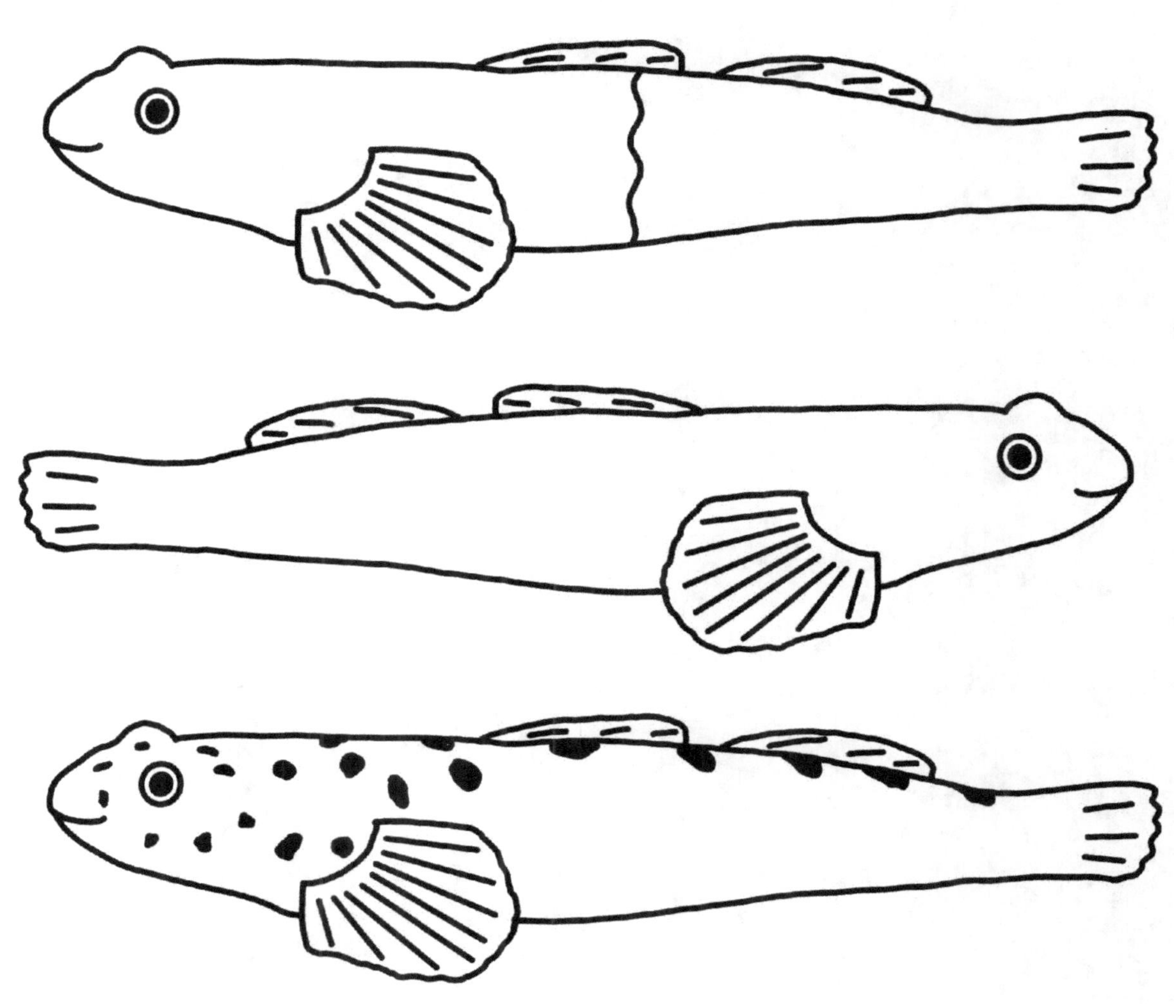

'O'OPU

'ALAMO'O

HAWAIIAN HONEY CREEPER

'AKIAPŌLĀ'AU

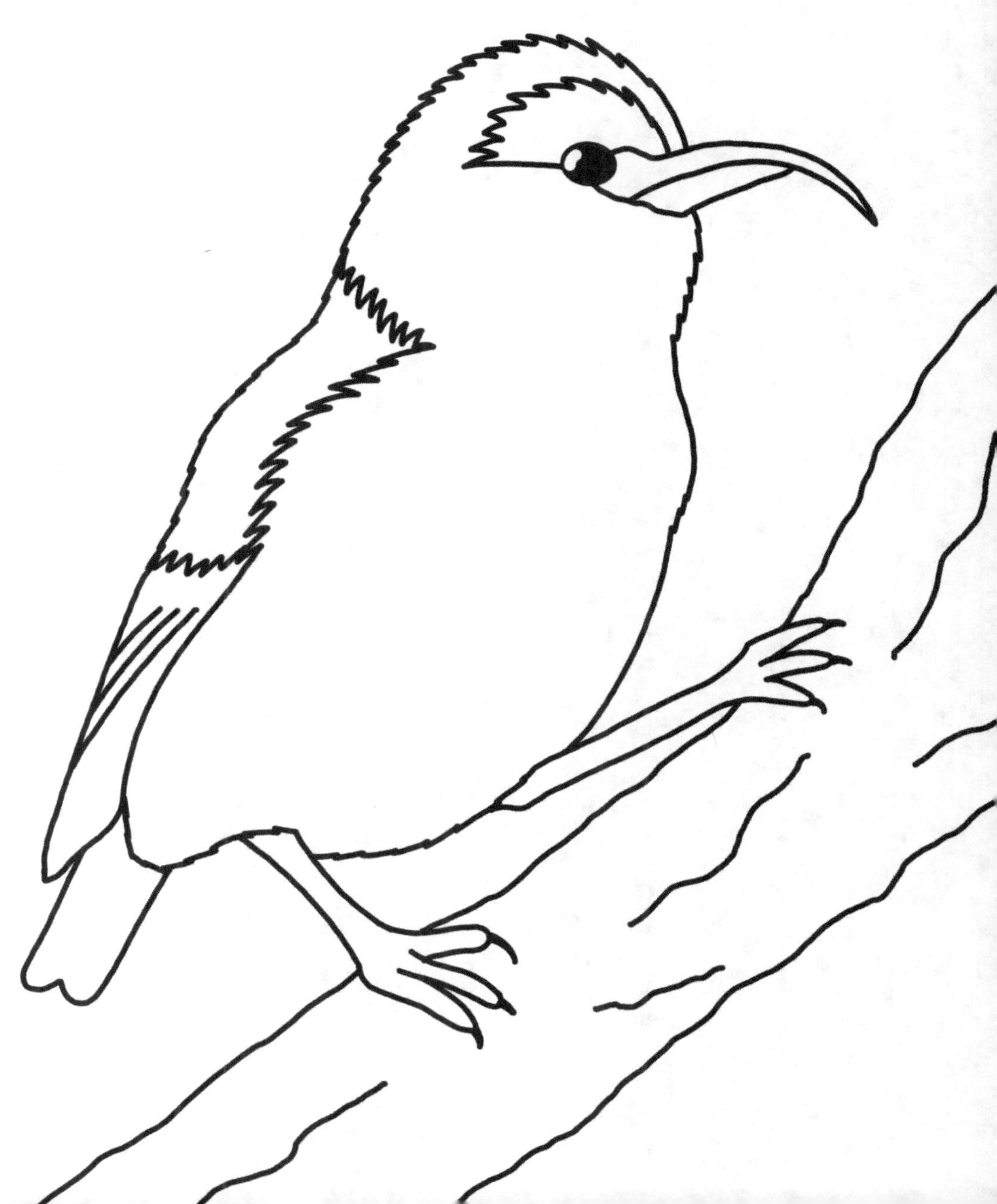

YELLOW-FACED BEE

NALO MELI

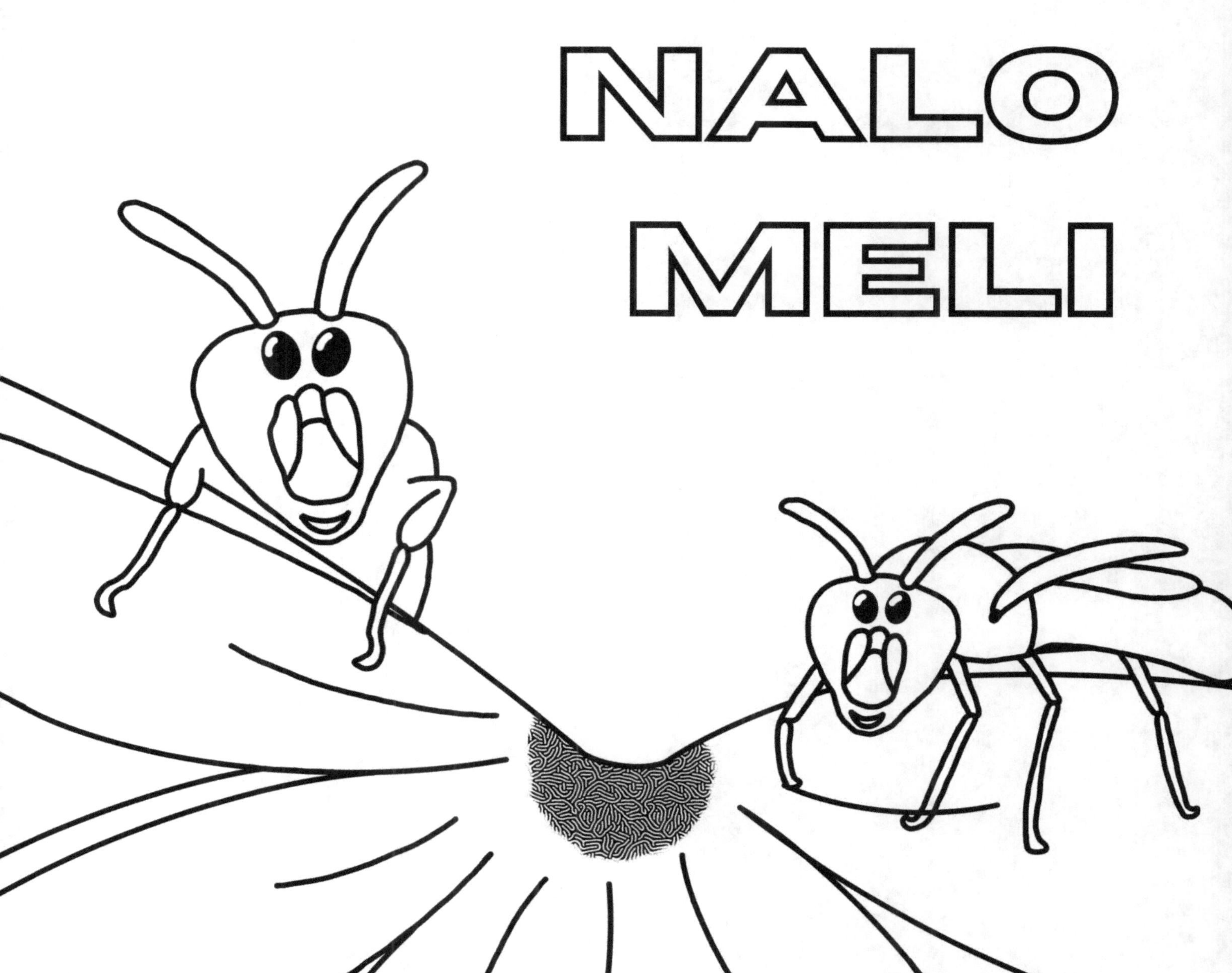

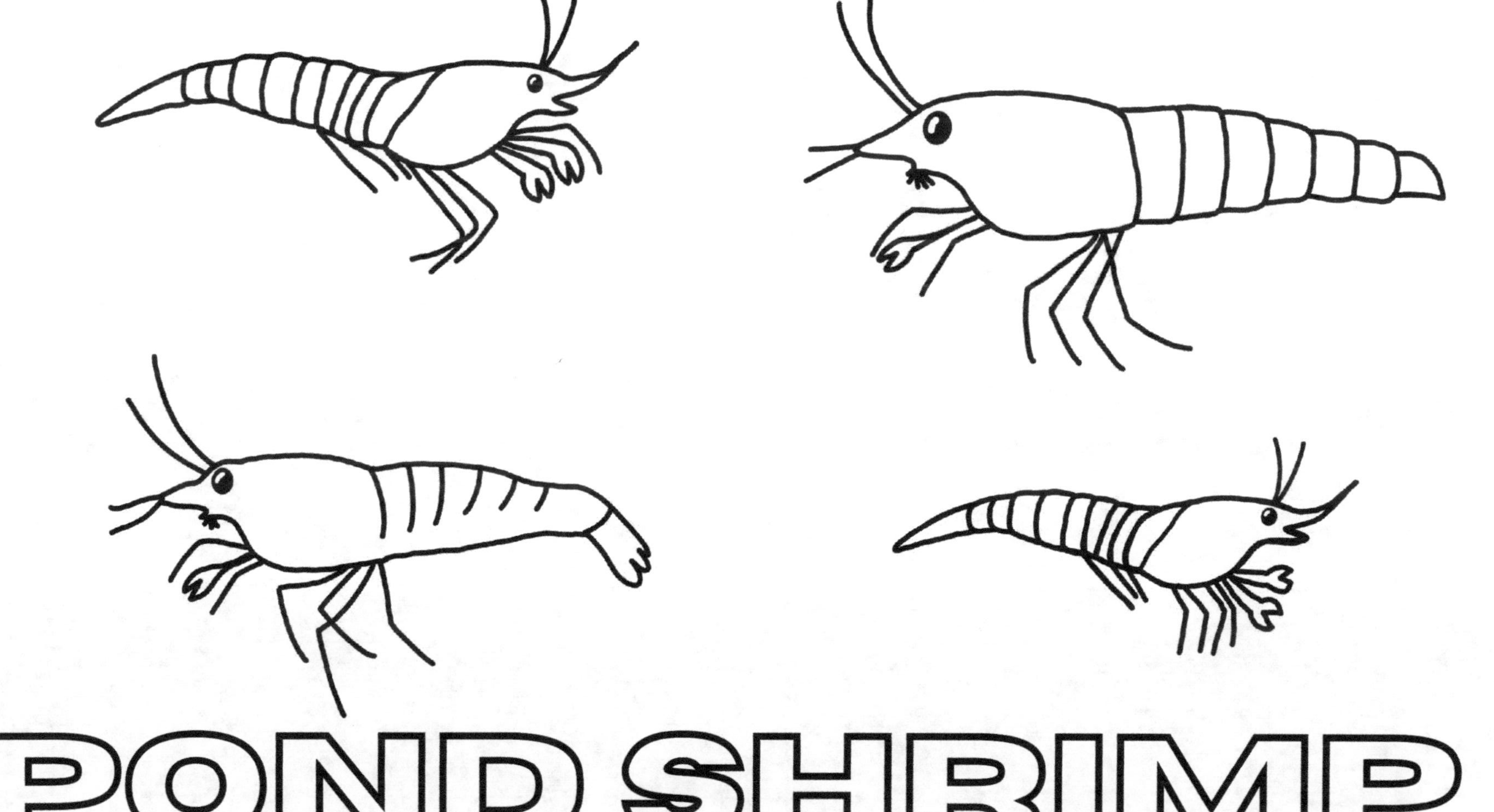
'ŌPAE 'ULA
POND SHRIMP

HAWAI'I THRUSH

'ŌMA'O

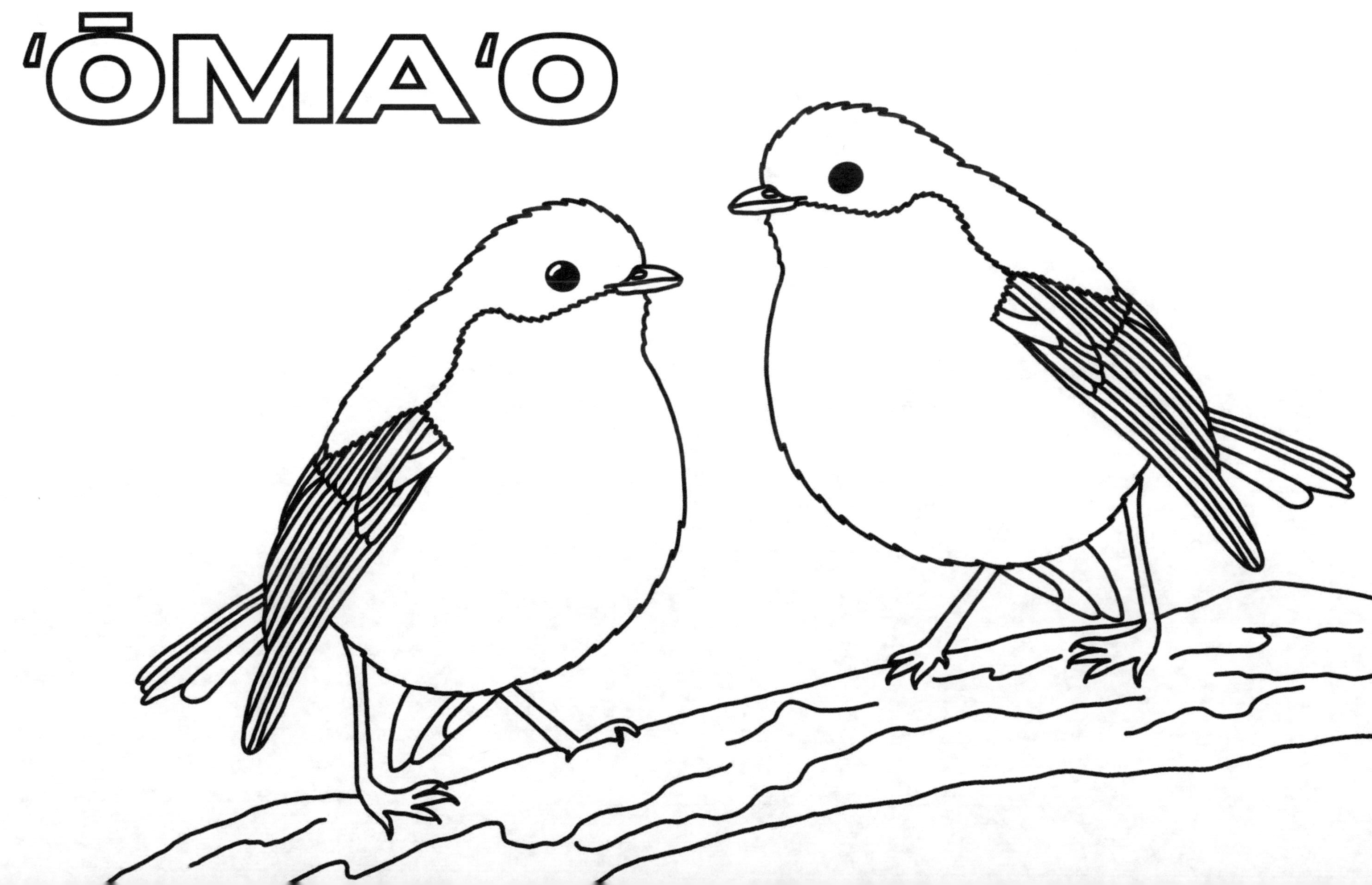

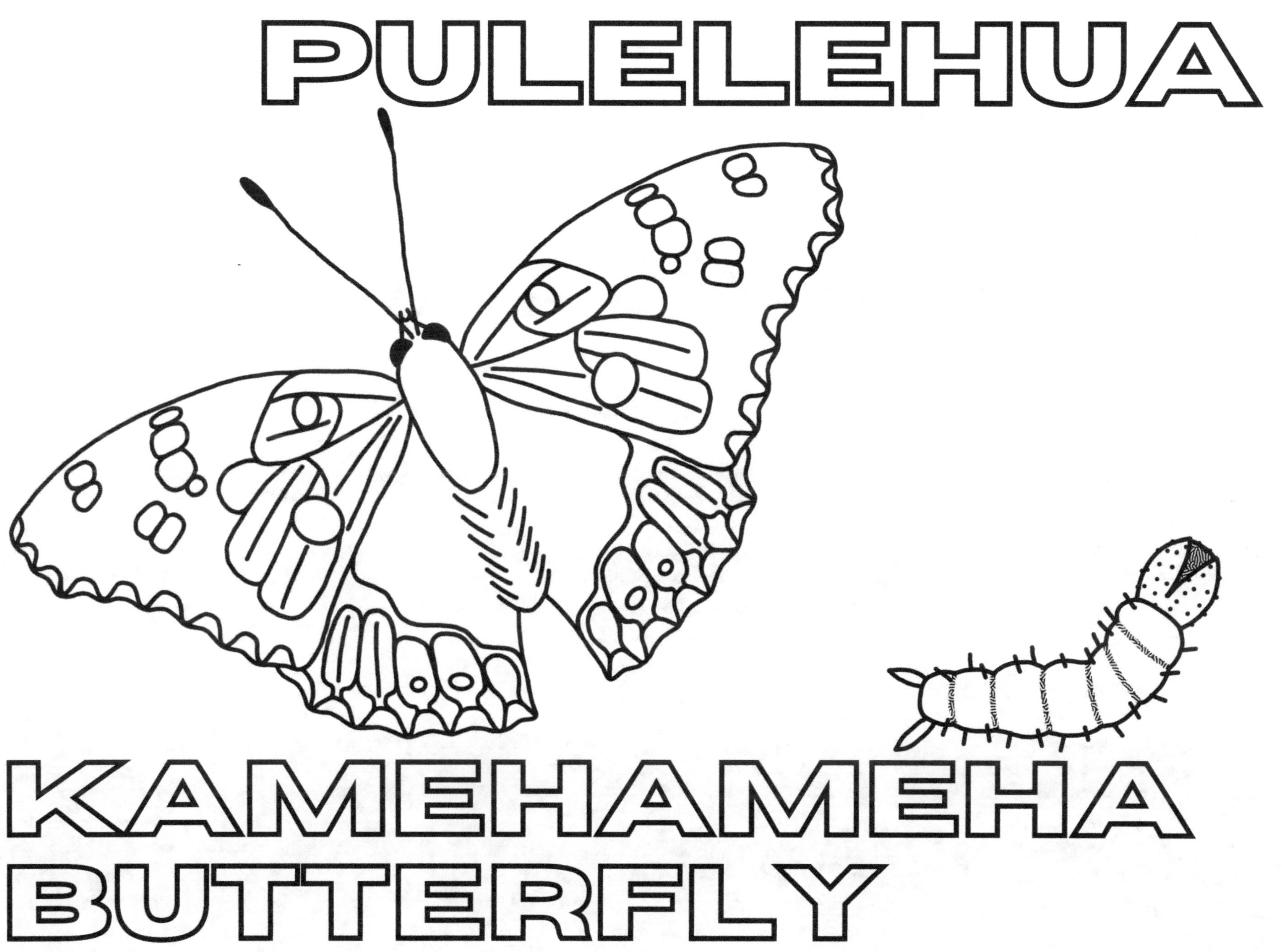

PULELEHUA
KAMEHAMEHA
BUTTERFLY

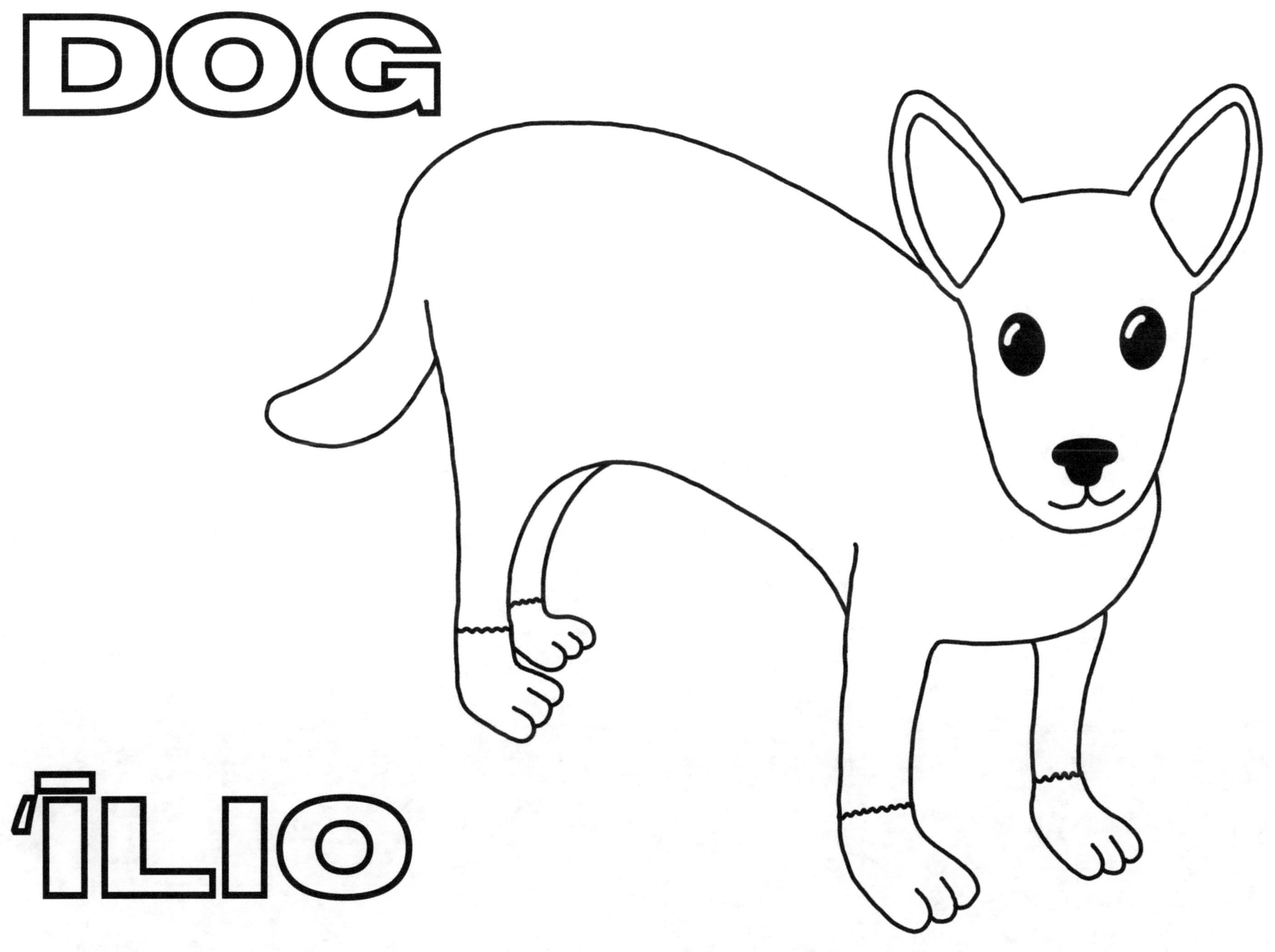

DOG
ÍLIO

MŌLĪ
LAYSAN
ALBATROSS

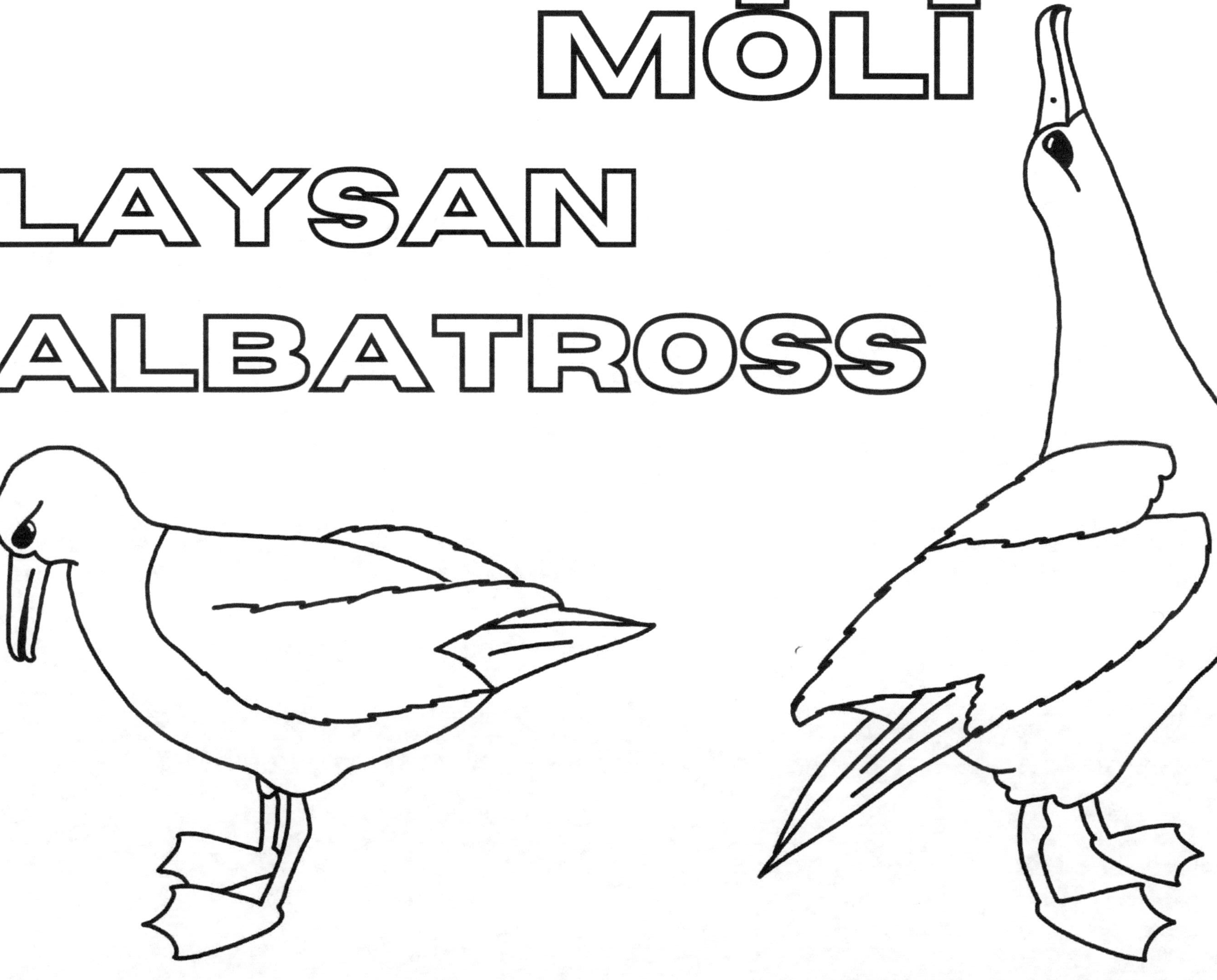

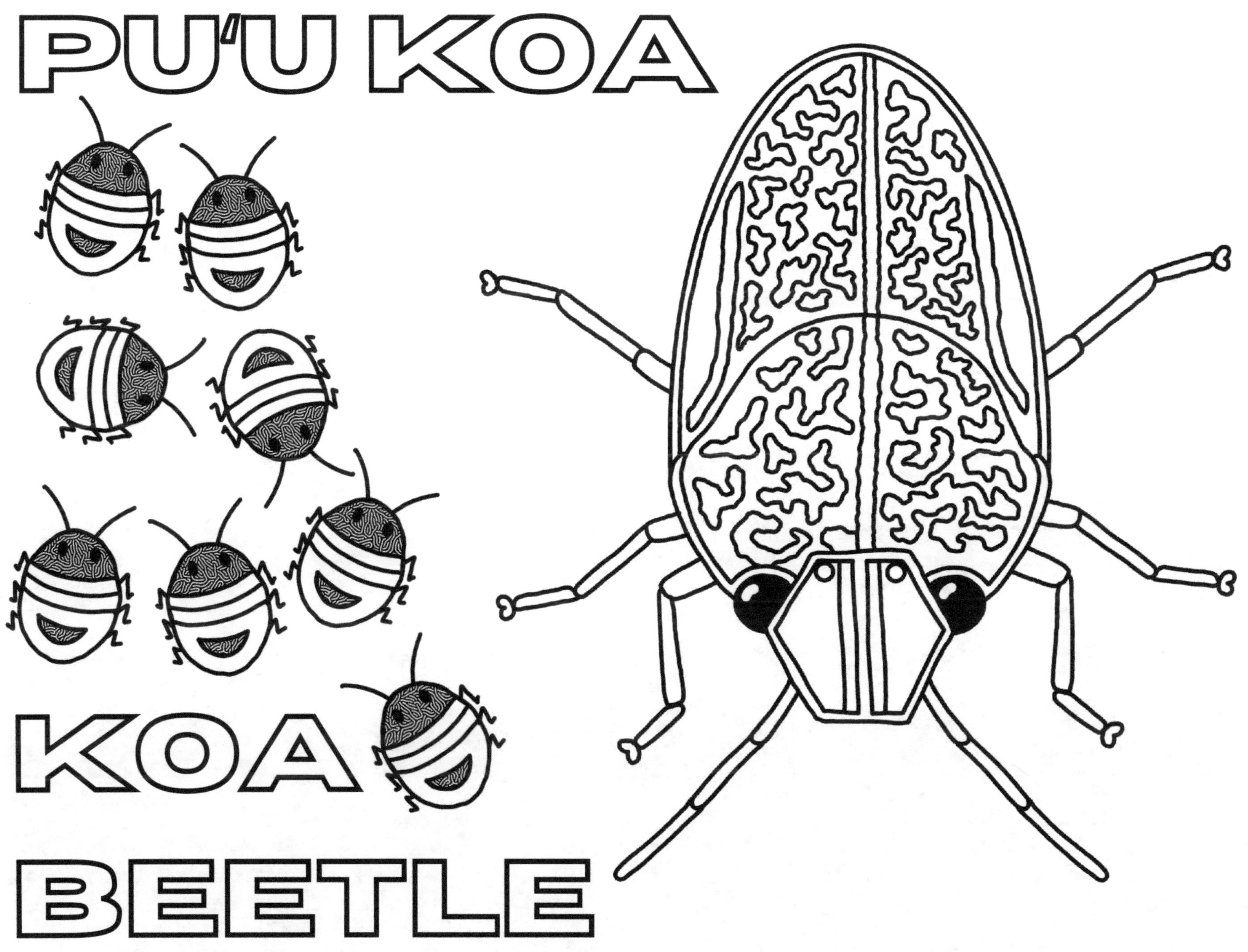

PU'U KOA
KO'A BEETLE

'ALAE KE'OKE'O

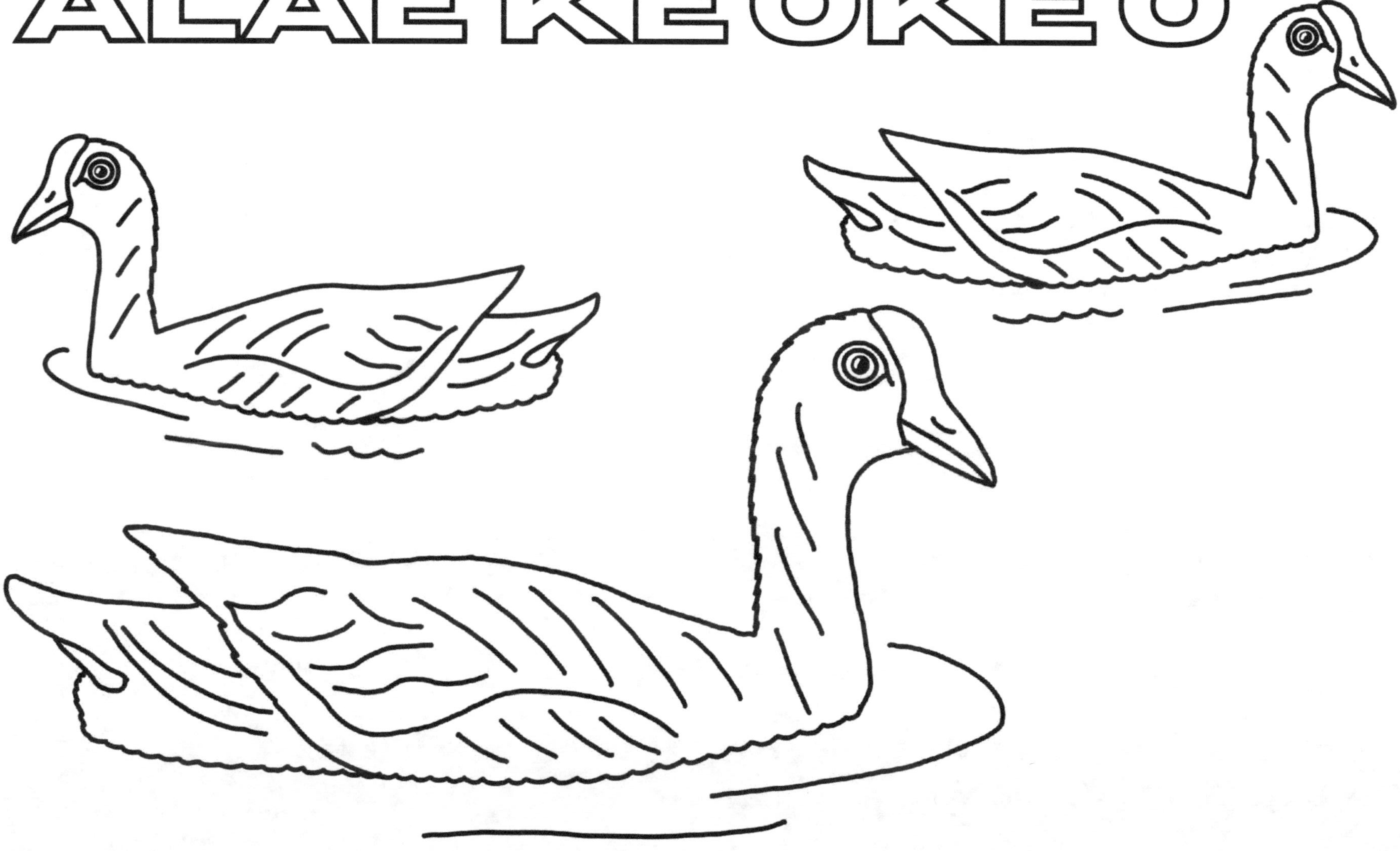

HAWAIIAN COOT

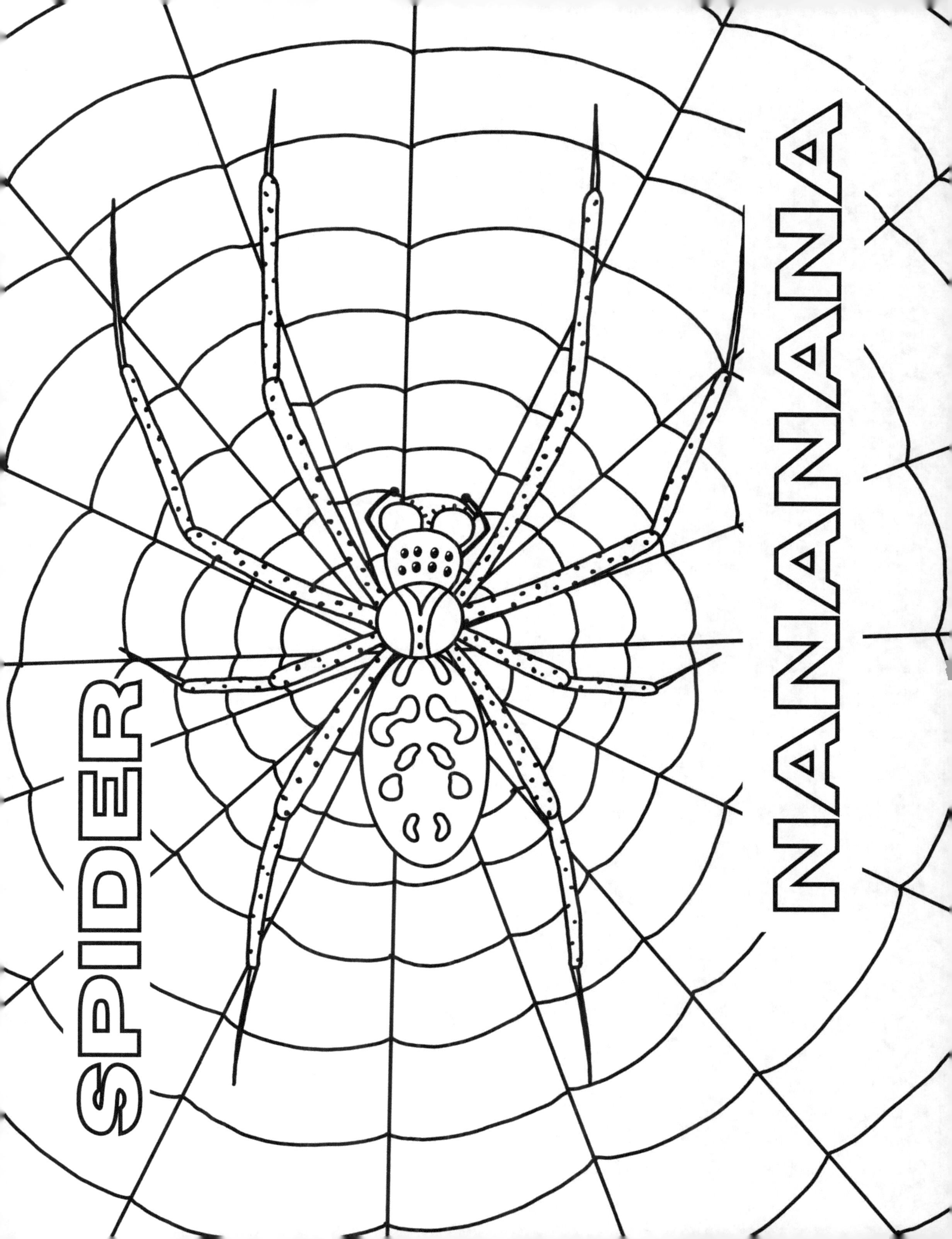

SPIIDER
NANANANA

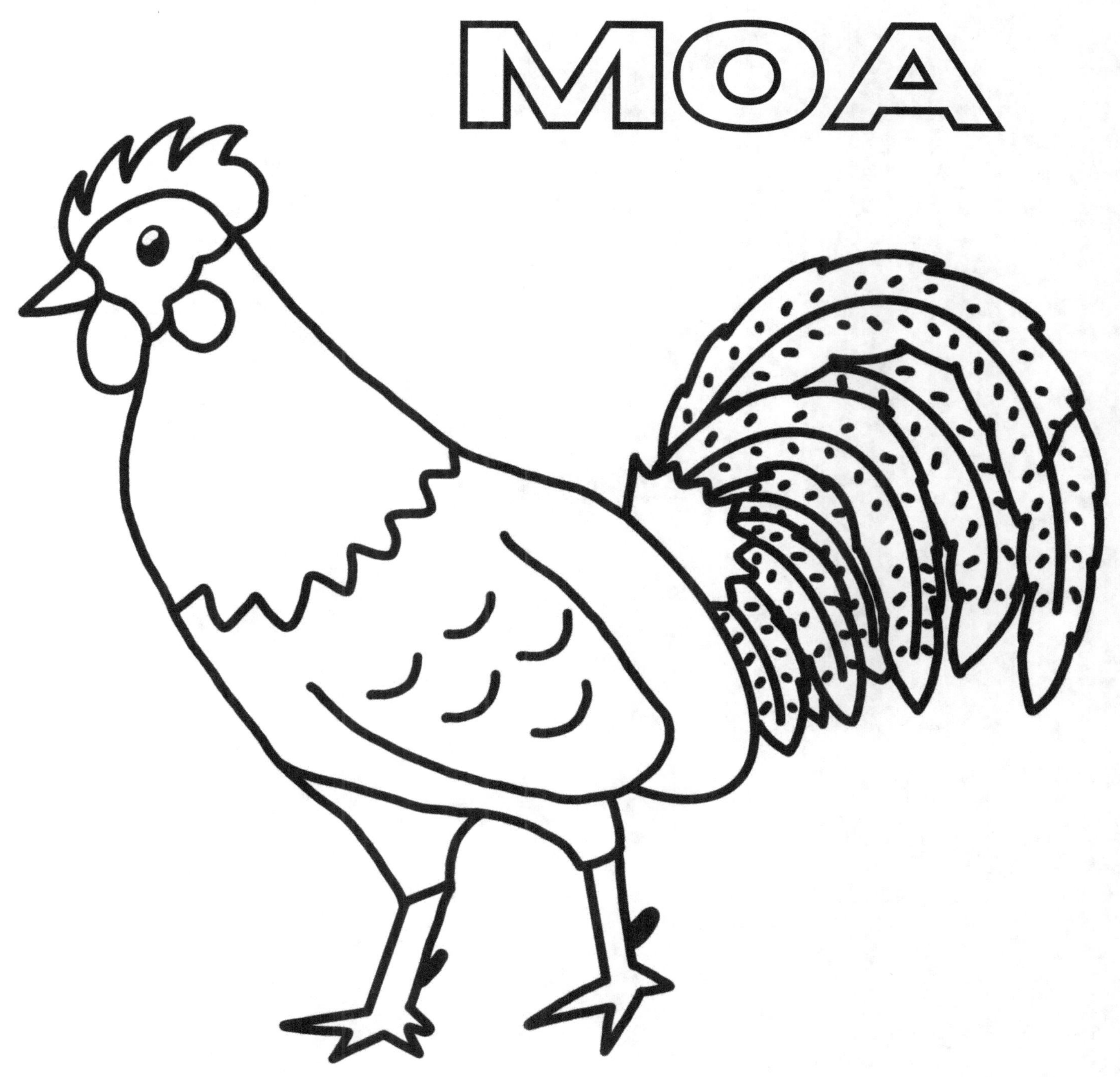

MOA
CHICKEN

HAWAIIAN STILT

AE'O

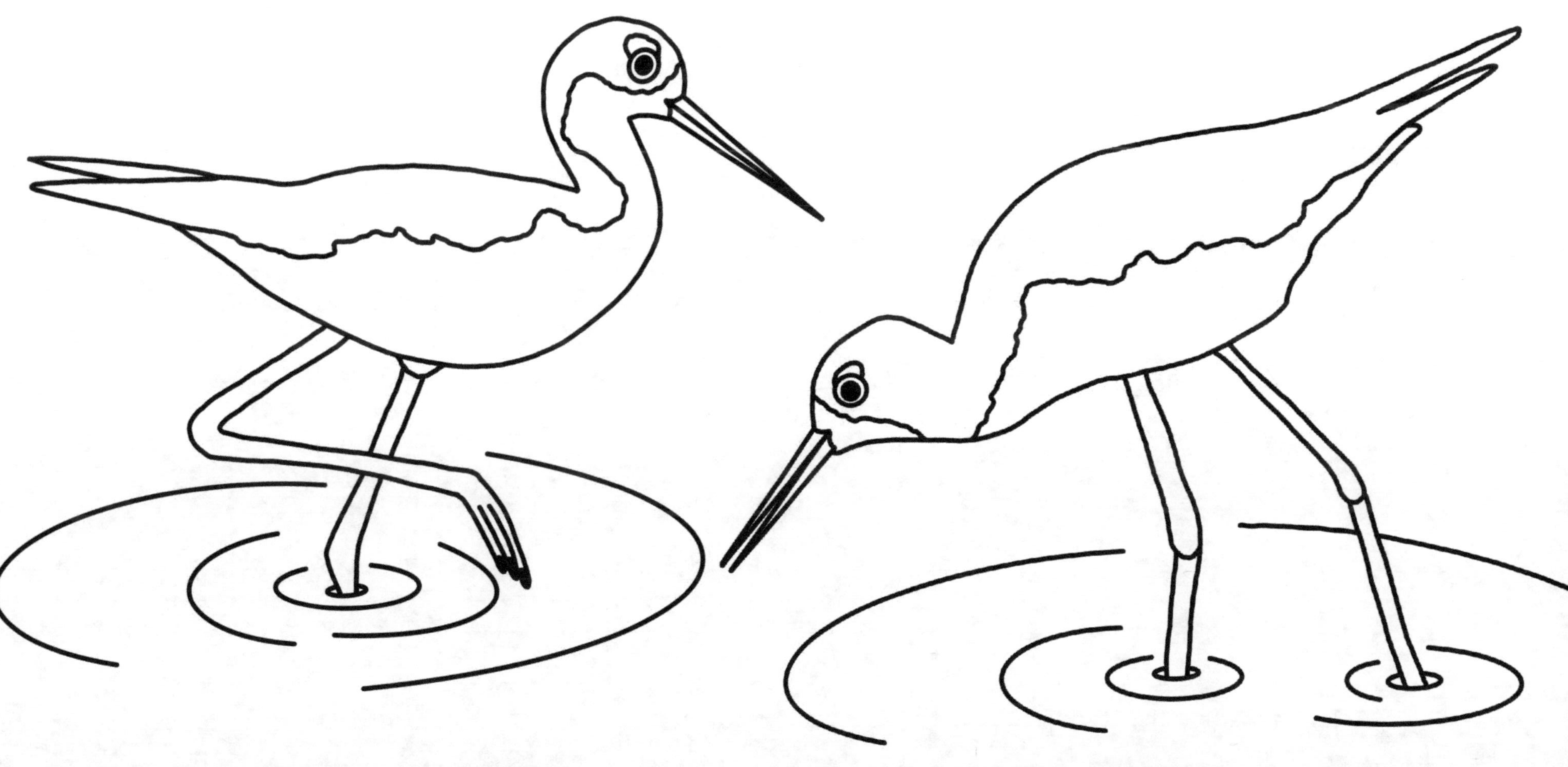

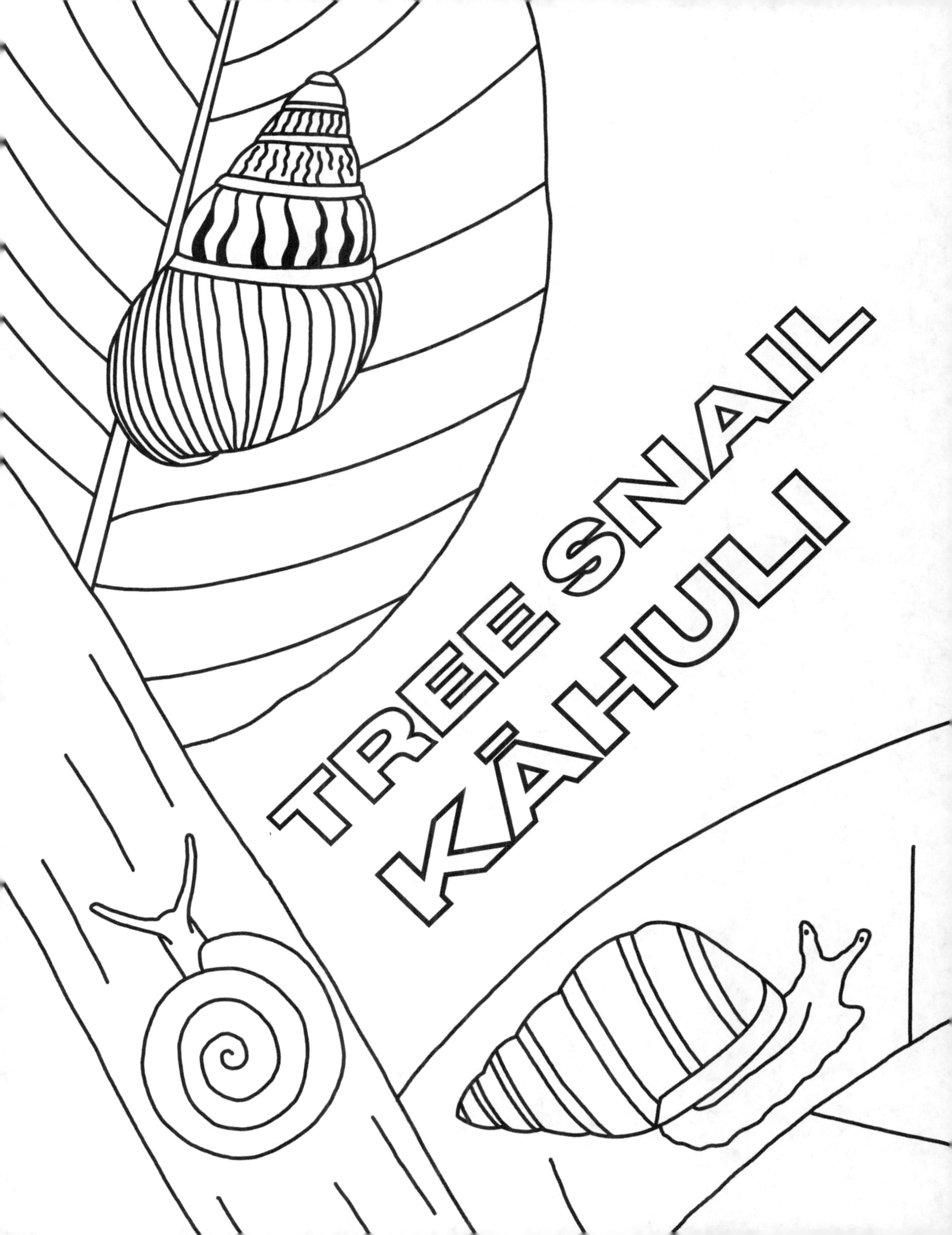

TREE SNAIL
KĀHULI

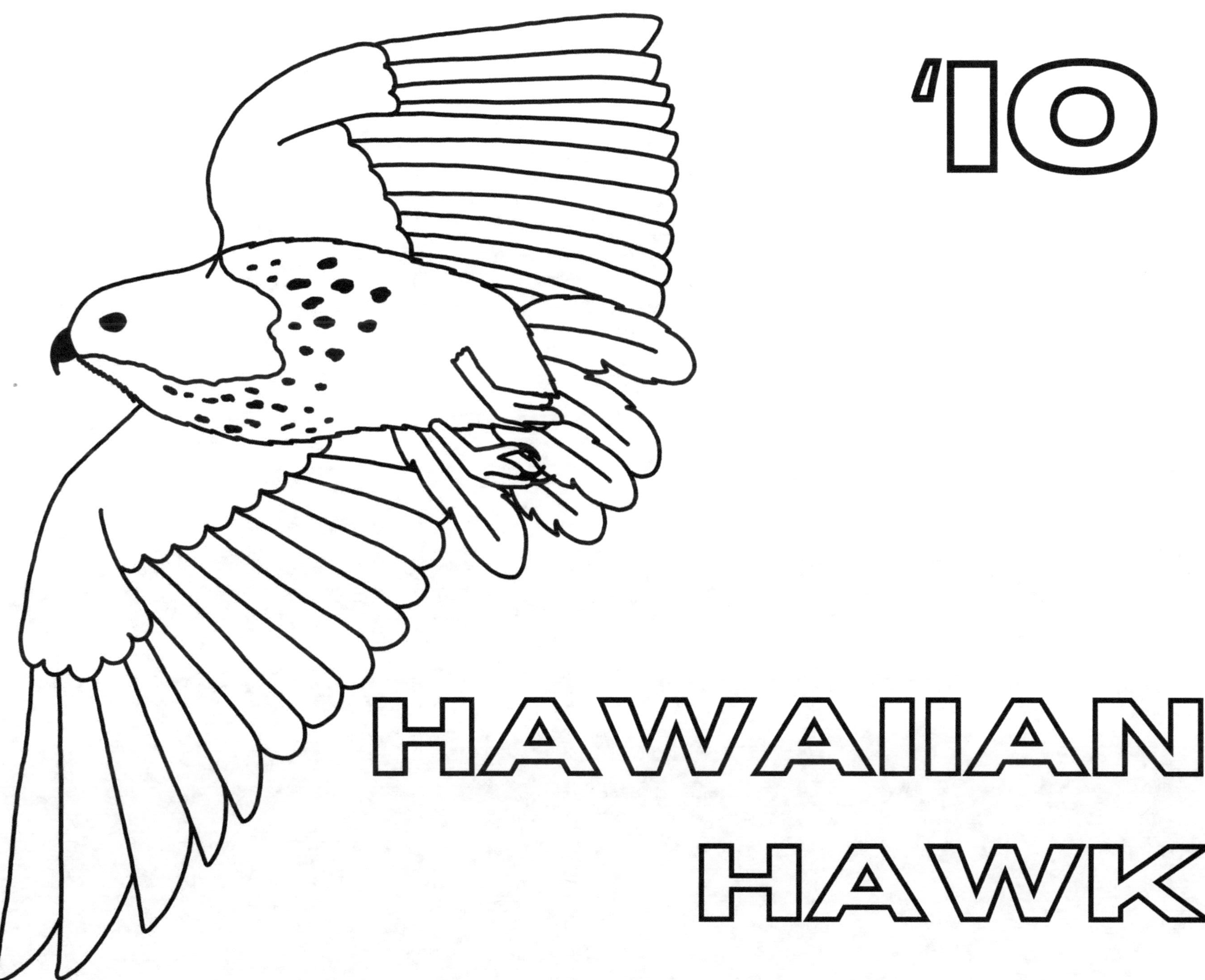
'IO
HAWAIIAN HAWK

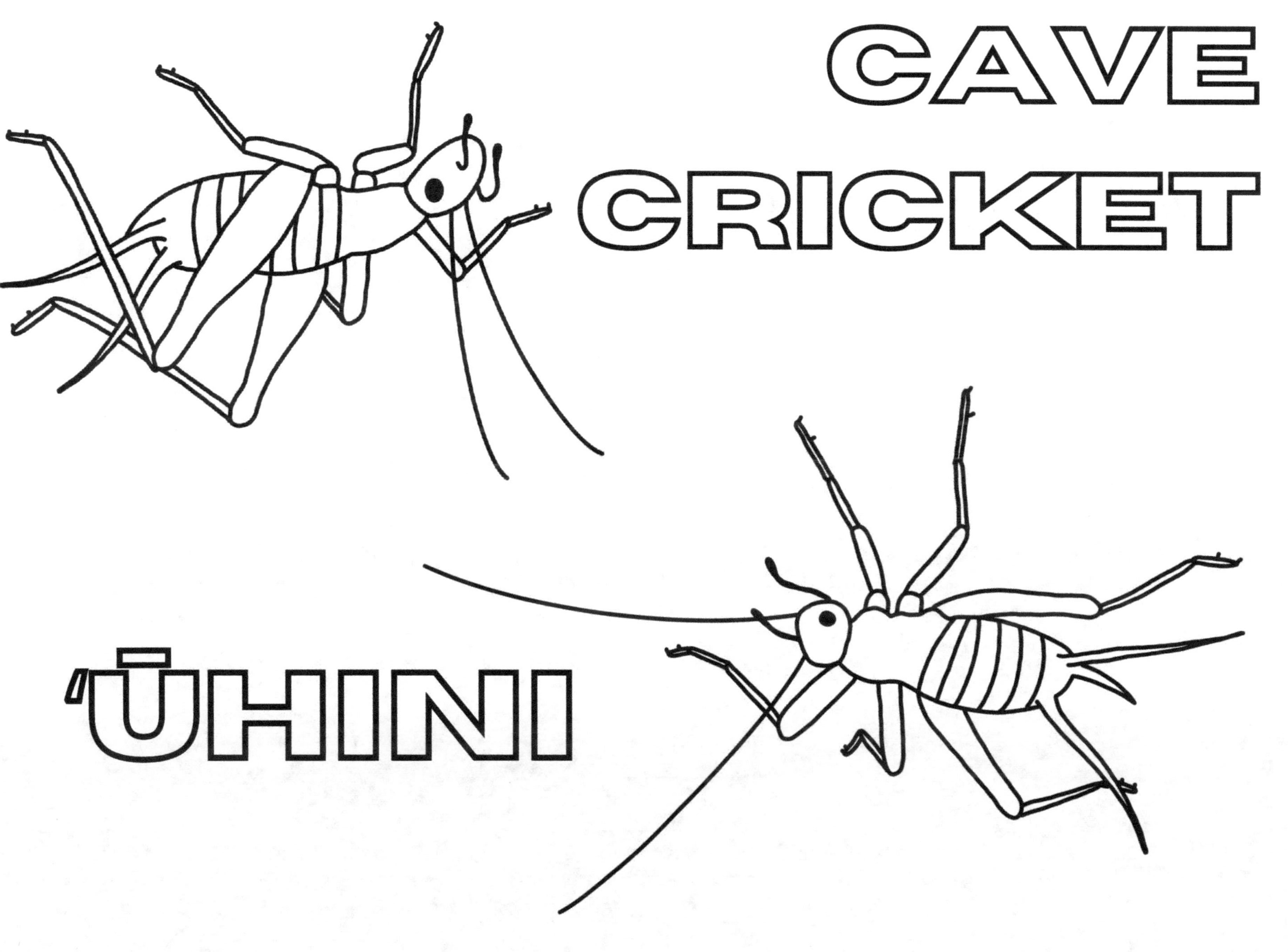

CAVE CRICKET
ʻŪHINI

PIG

PUA‘A

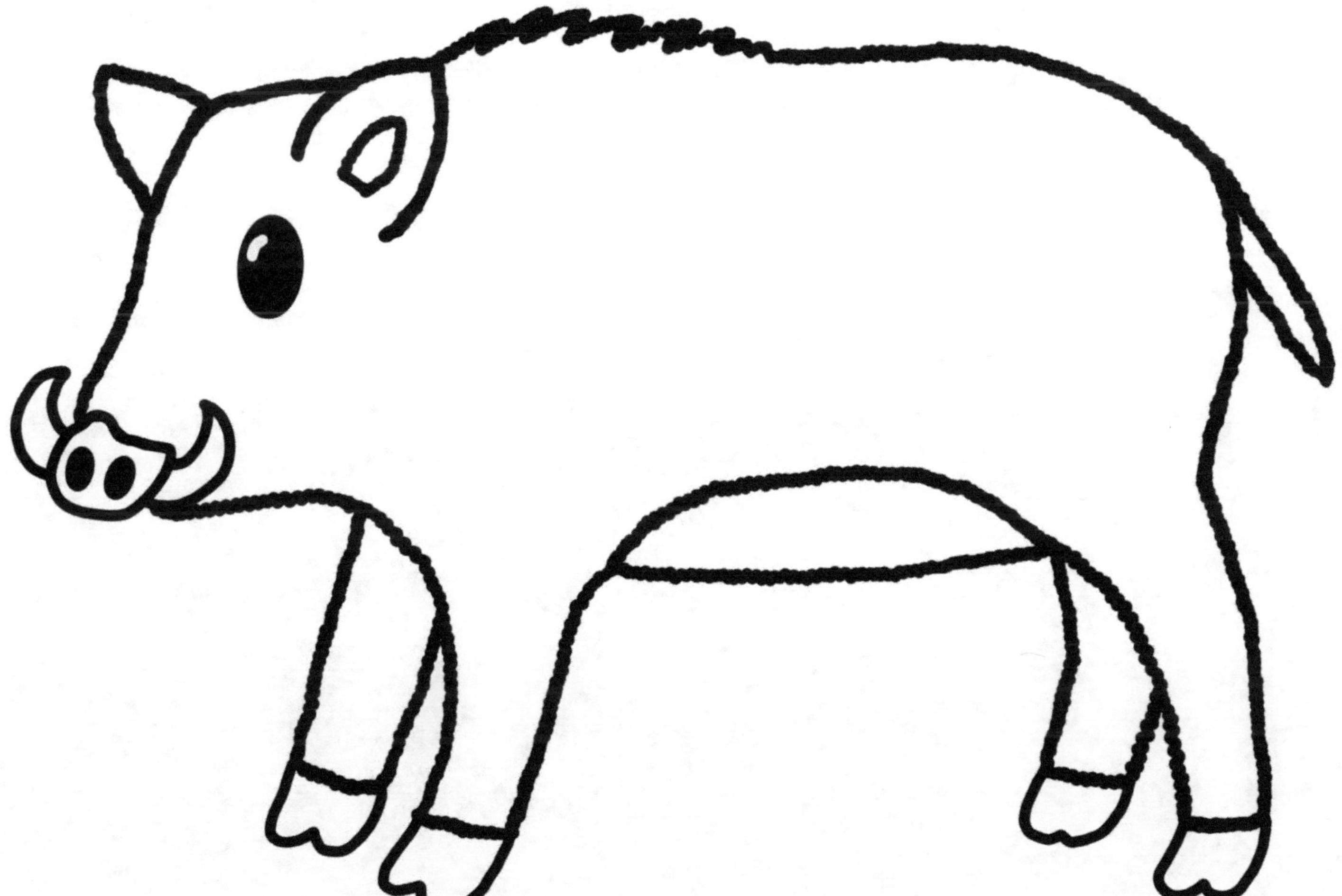

PUEO

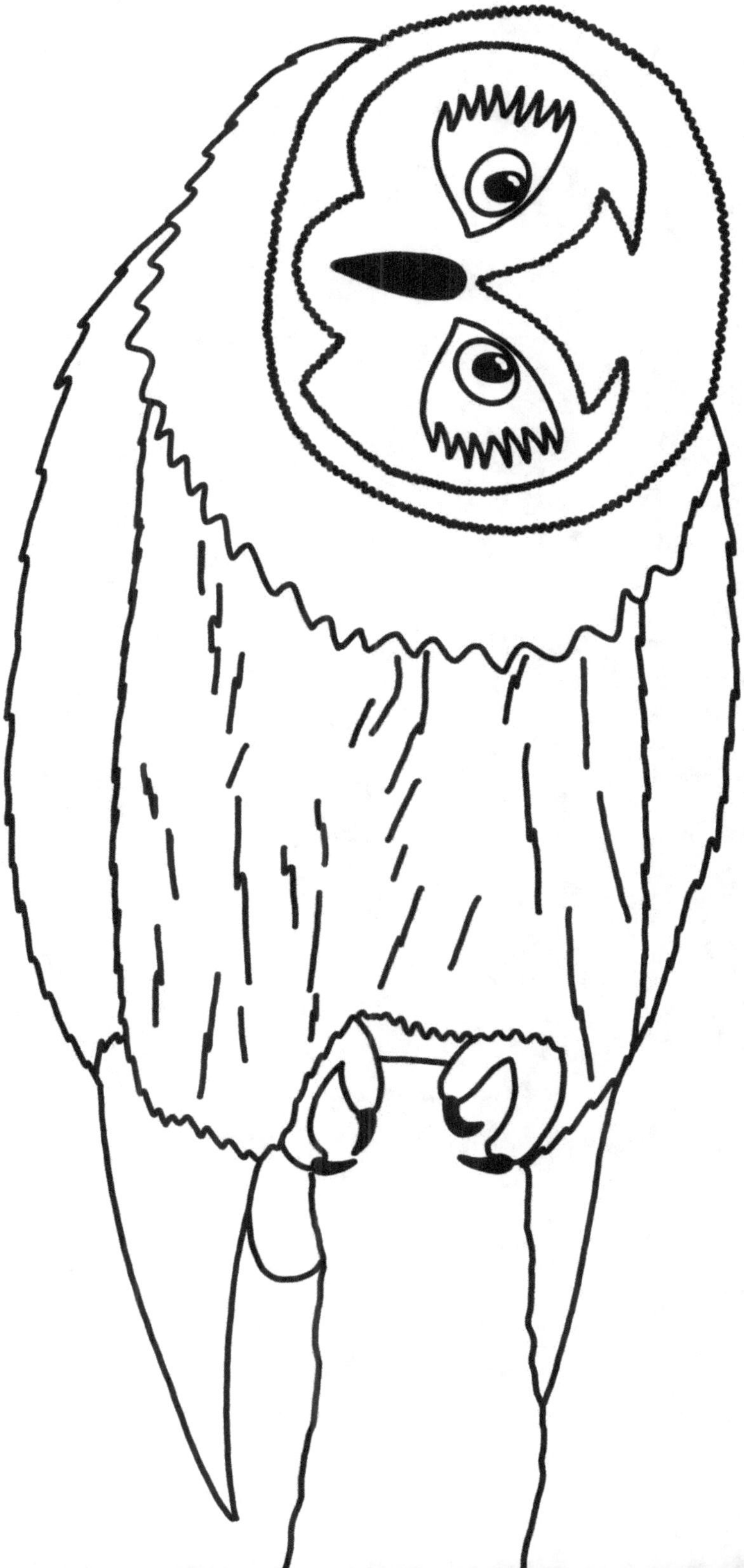

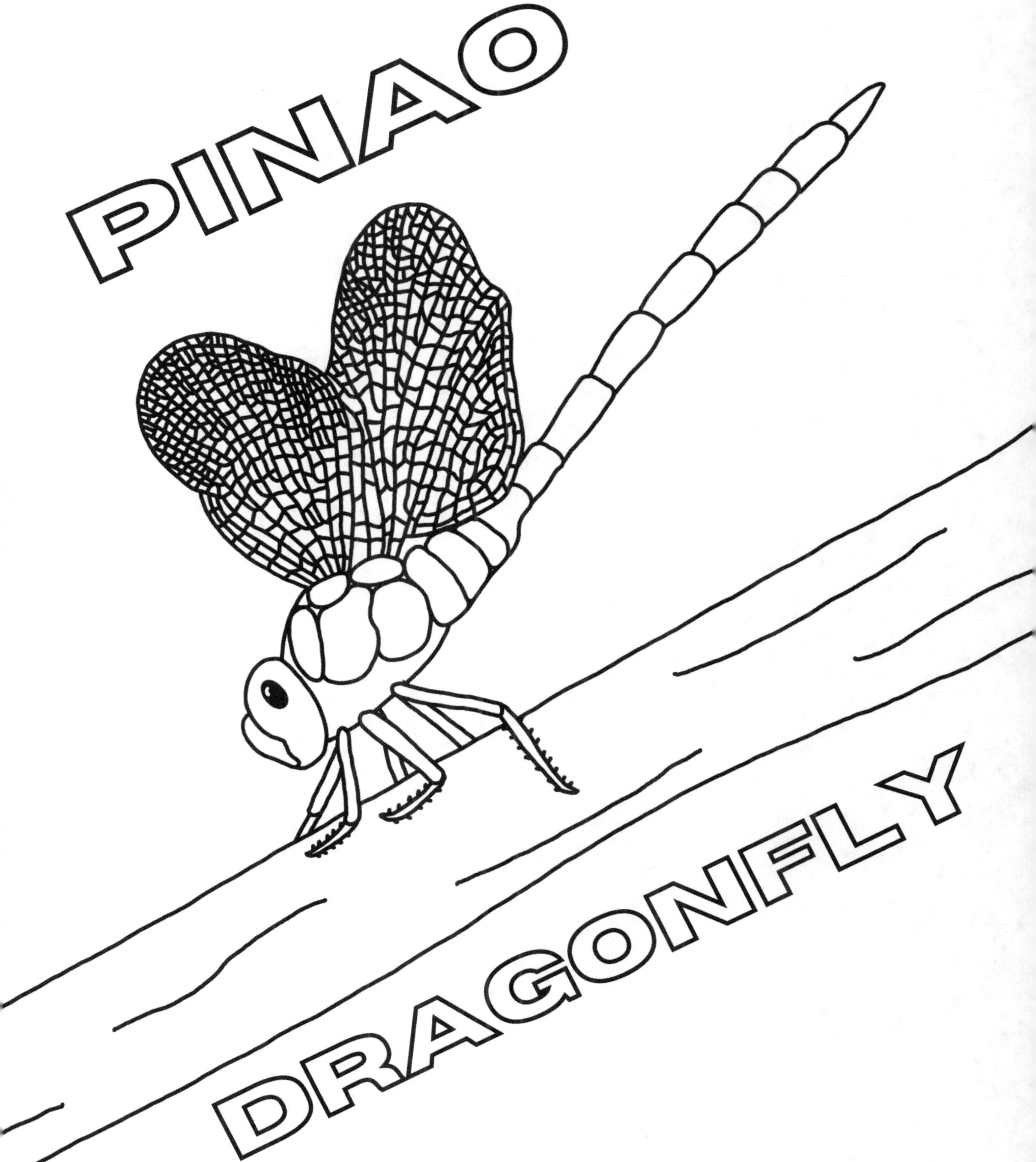

PINAO
DRAGONFLY

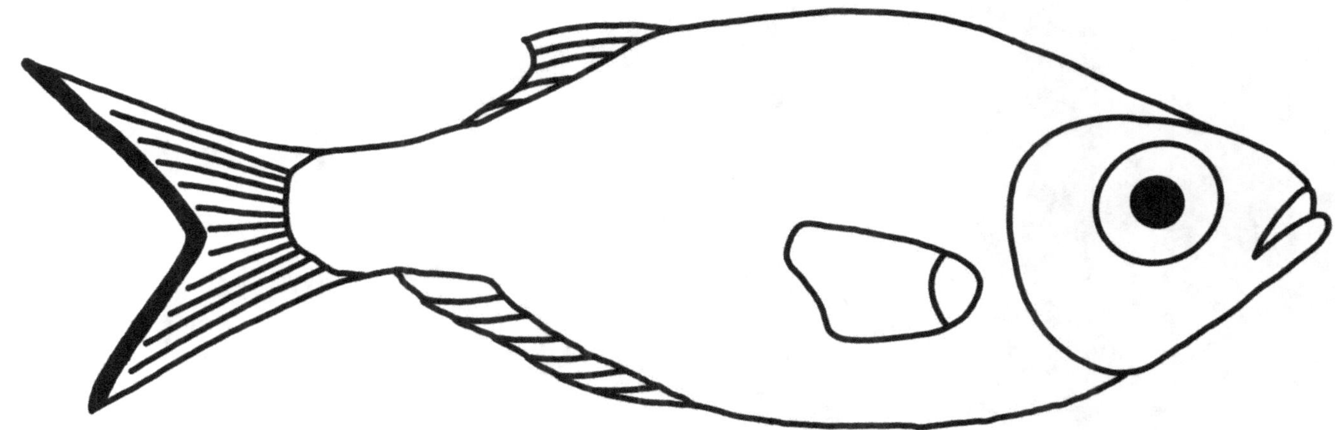

ĀHOLEHOLE

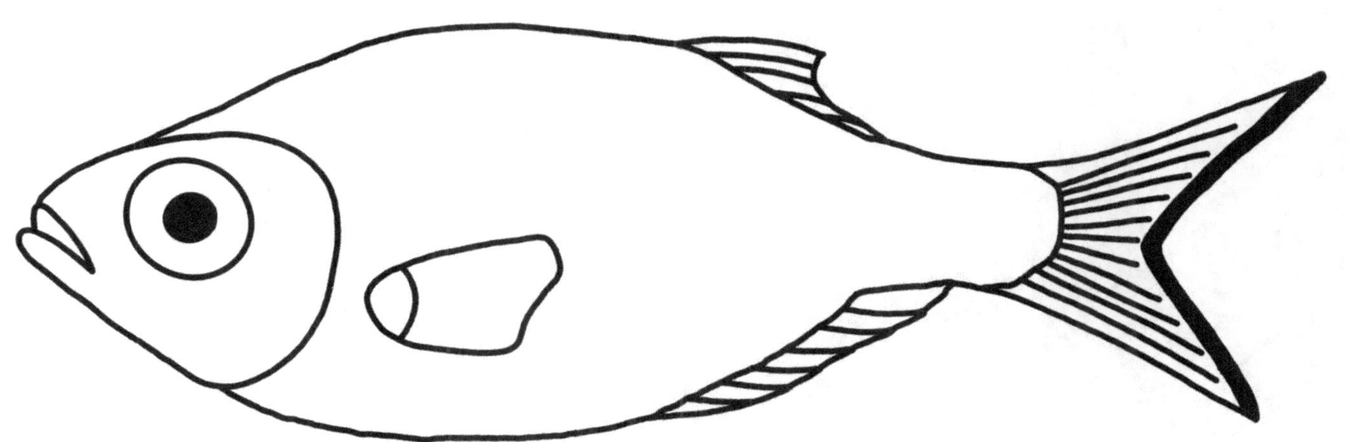

FLAGTAIL

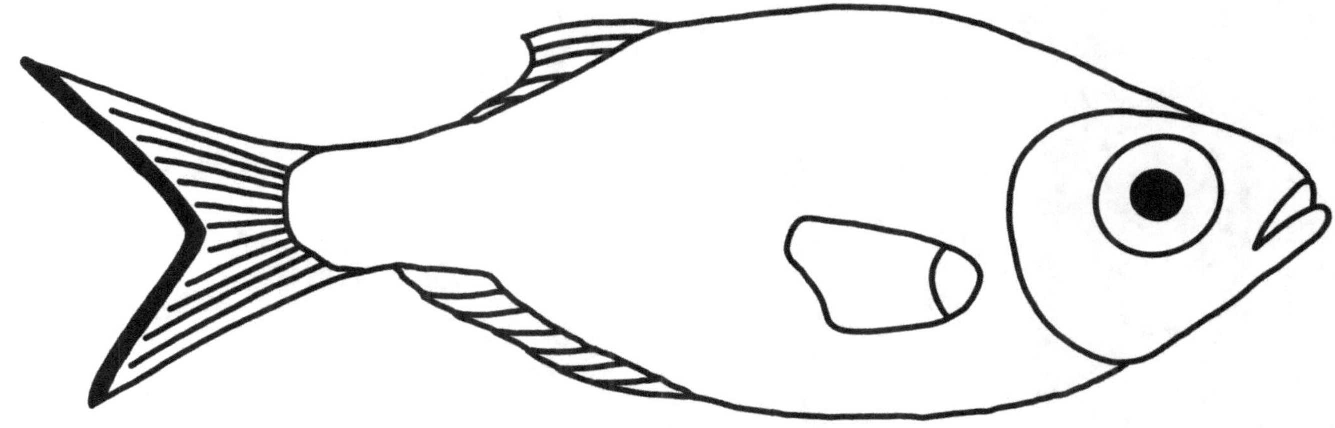

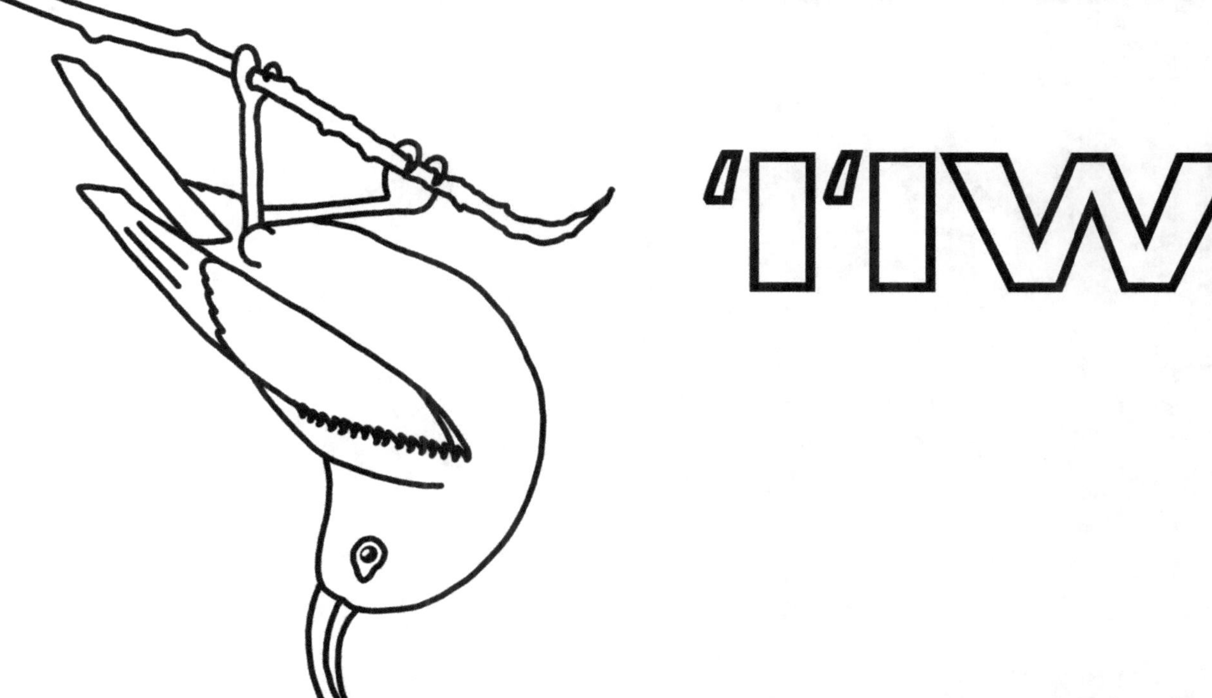

'I'IWI

SCARLET HAWAIIAN HONEY CREEPER

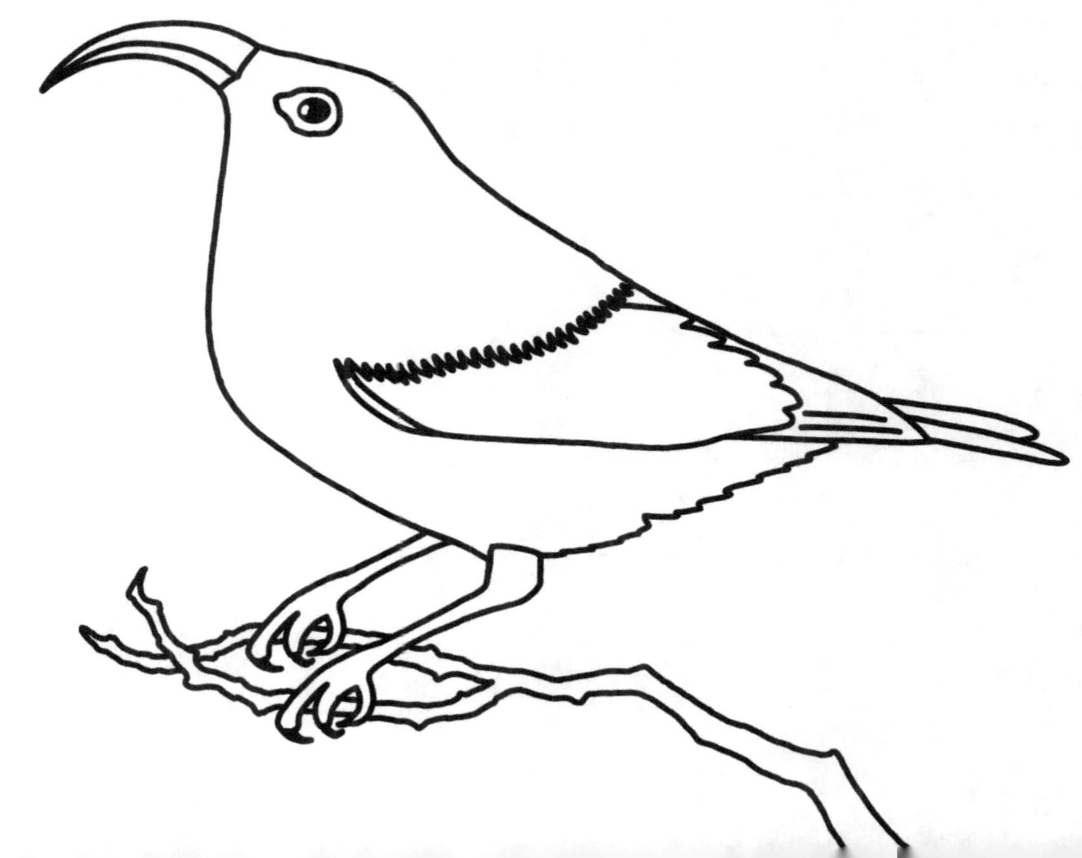

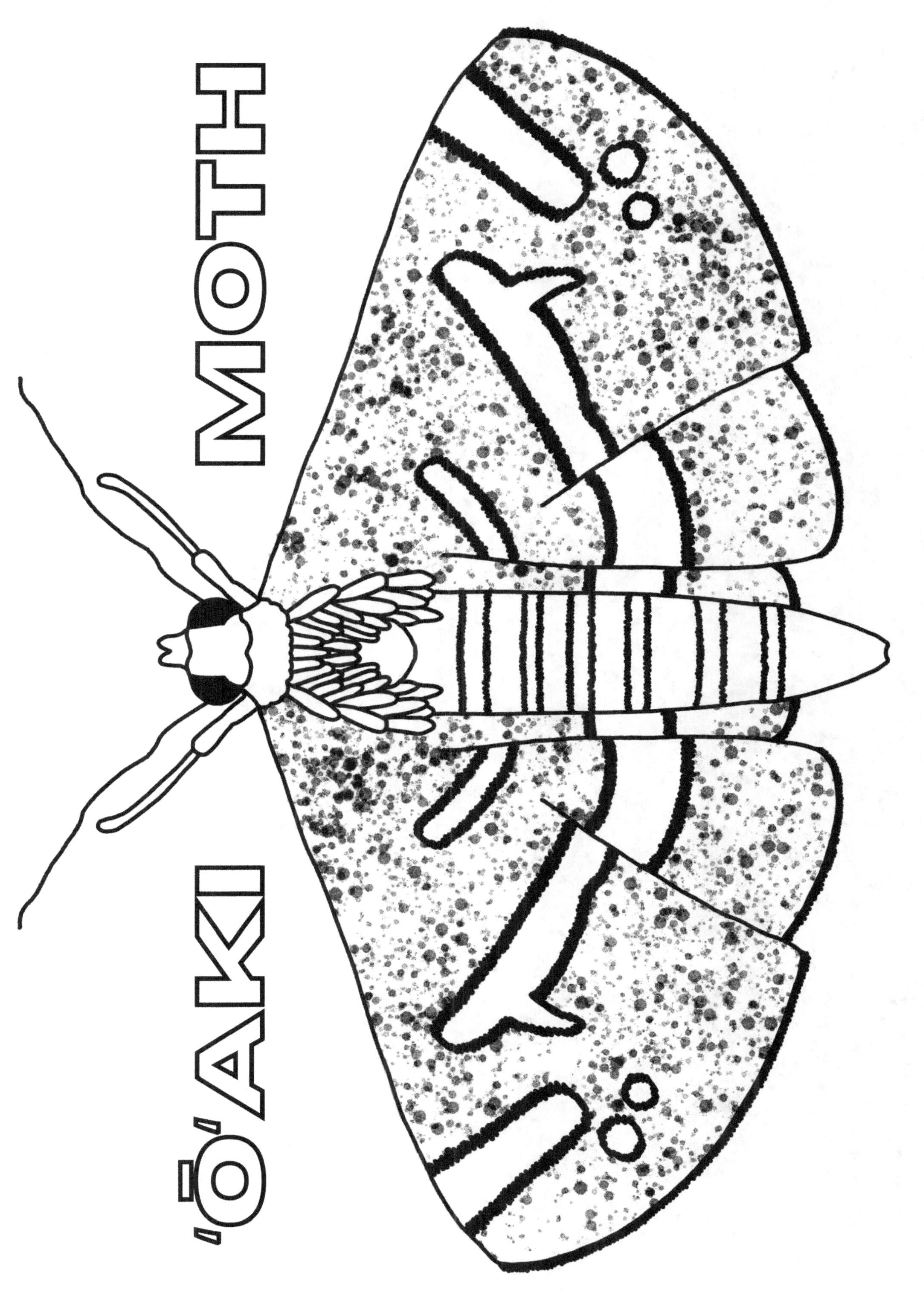

MOTH
'Ō'AKI

HAWAIIAN GOOSE

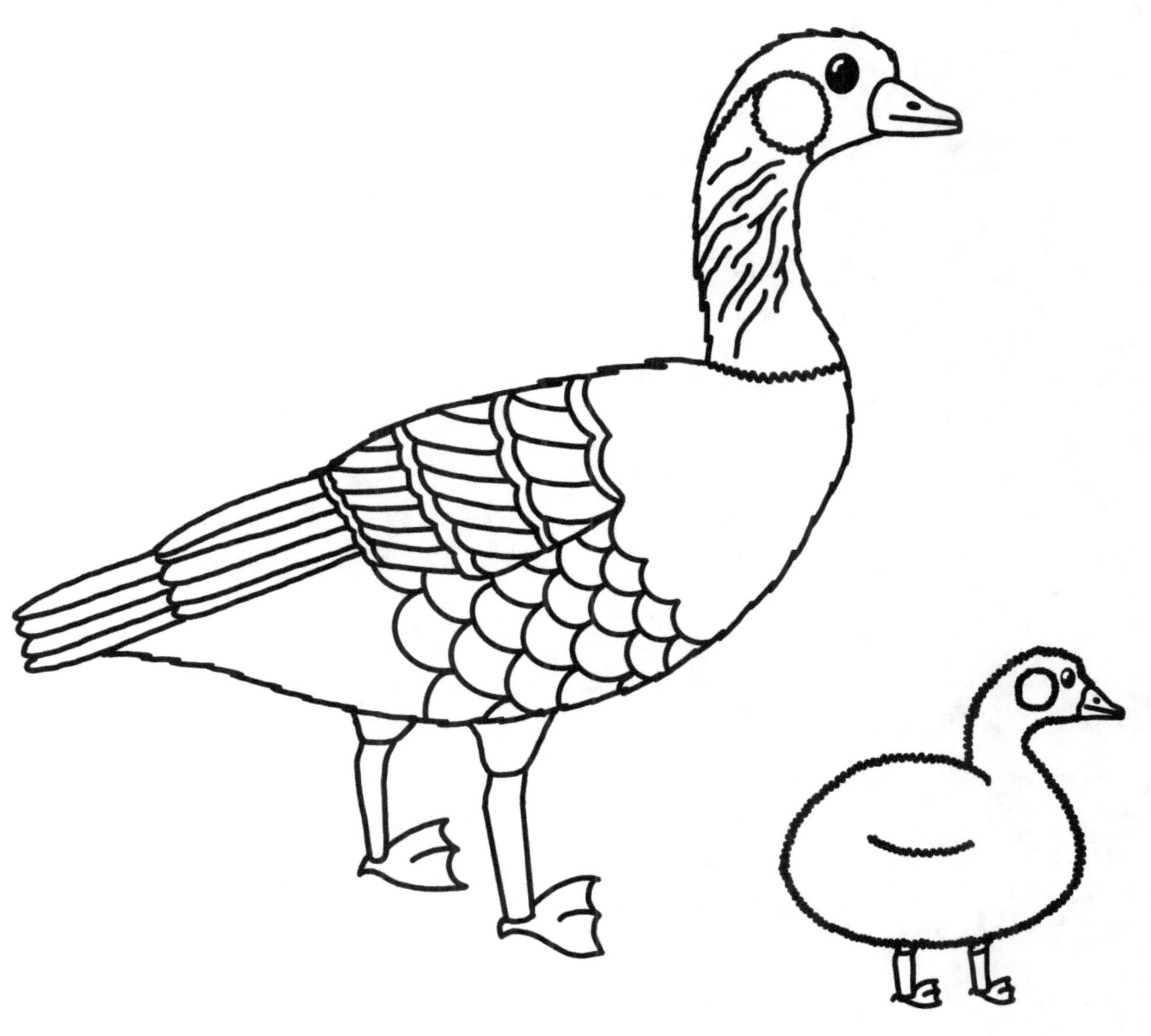

NĒNĒ

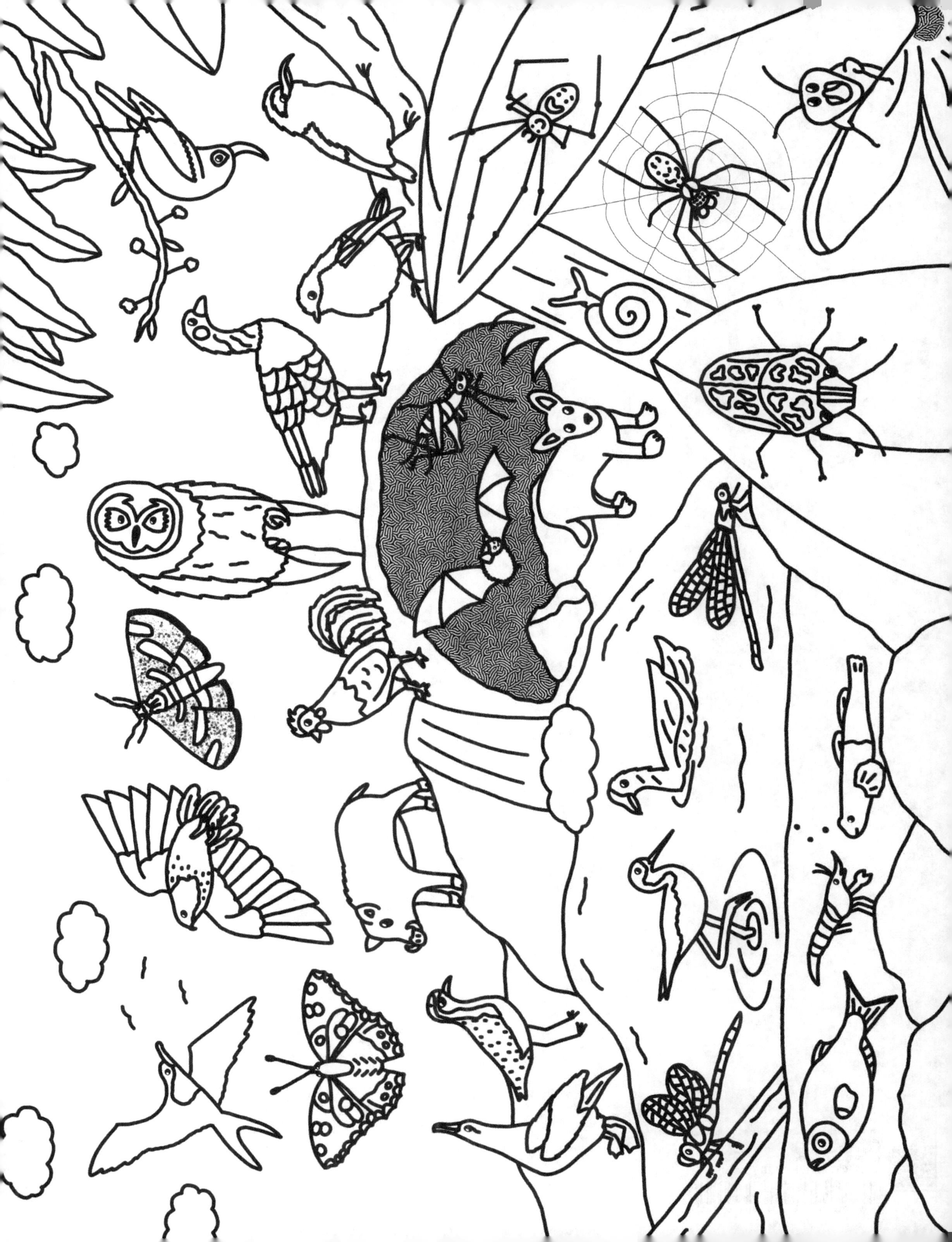